Debbie Travis' Facelift
Solutions to Revitalize Your Home

Debbie Travis with Barbara Dingle

Clarkson Potter/Publishers
New York

To my two young men,
Josh and Max,
who are simply the best.

Amazing Hans,
forever by my side.
Thanks.

Copyright © 2005 by Debbie Travis

Photograph Credits
George Ross: pages 6, 7, 20–29, 50–59, 76–85, 108–17, 141, 142 (top), 144–53.
Manon Boyer: pages 1, 2, 8, 9, 12–19, 30, 31 (left), 32 (right), 33–37, 38 (center),
39–45, 60–63, 64 (top), 65–67, 72–75, 86–89, 90 (top), 91–93, 98–107, 118–21, 123–37,
139, 142 (bottom), 154, 155 (top), 157–59. Joe Oliveira: pages 31 (right), 46 (left),
47–49, 68 (left), 69, 70, 94 (left), 95, 96 (top), 97, 155 (bottom). All other
photographs are candids belonging to Facelift Productions or are AVID
still shots taken directly from an episode of *Debbie Travis' Facelift.*

Cover Credits: Cover photography by Dan Lim
Stylist: Rachel Mathews
Wardrobe: Holt Renfrew

Published by Clarkson Potter/Publishers, New York, New York.
Member of the Crown Publishing Group, a division of Random House, Inc.
www.crownpublishing.com

CLARKSON N. POTTER is a trademark and POTTER and colophon are registered
trademarks of Random House, Inc.

Printed in China

Design by Jan Derevjanik

Library of Congress Cataloging-in-Publication Data
Travis, Debbie.
Debbie Travis' facelift : solutions to revitalize your home / Debbie Travis with
Barbara Dingle ; main photography by George Ross.— 1st ed.
p. cm.
Includes index.
1. House painting. 2. Color in interior decoration. I. Title: Facelift. II. Dingle,
Barbara. III. Title.
TT323.T6922 2004   747'.94—dc22   2004019432

ISBN: 1-4000-8153-X

1 3 5 7 9 10 8 6 4 2

First Edition

acknowledgments

For me, whacking down walls, ripping out kitchens, and choosing color schemes is not incredibly stressful. On the other hand, the discipline of writing is an endless challenge. Without Barb Dingle, my writer *extraordinaire,* you would not be enjoying this book. She badgers me relentlessly, tidies up my prose, and supplies constant motivation. **Thanks, Barb.**

A picture tells a thousand stories, and it is the inspiring photographs in this book that reveal the passion we have for our homes. George Ross, my dear friend, has an eye for beautiful spaces, color, and texture. He manages to transfer all our hard work onto the page with splendor and elegance. Manon Boyer's photography of the *Facelift* team at work captures the excitement of our jobs perfectly. **Thanks, George and Manon.**

Anne Côté is a visionary, a talent who sees hope in the most desperate room. No space is too ugly for Anne's imagination. Anne's skill as an art director is unsurpassed, and the whole team and every homeowner are constantly surprised and delighted with the results of the Facelifts. **Thanks, Anne.**

These Facelifts are not just spectacular renovations, they are also successful television shows. *Facelift* is about good design, but it is also a reality show; what you see on your television screen is all real. To achieve this, it takes someone with immense talent and high, high energy. Catherine Pilon is a brilliant director. She captures the drama of renovating along with the real-life stories of the homeowners in a way that is mesmerizing to watch. She turns a decorating show into an hour of breathtaking television. **Thanks, Catherine.**

Scott Bailey and Travis Champion are not only the coolest guys around, they must be the most hardworking. Never sitting down during our long days and nights, they are there to make these Facelifts happen in record time. But there is so much more to their roles. They will always be successes because of their ability to keep a busy and stressed team happy and smiling. **Thanks, Scott and Travis.**

The creative team is immense, and I would like to thank them all. Members of this incredible team of builders, carpenters, artists, painters, stylists, plumbers, and electricians have the most unusual jobs. Not only must they be the best at their craft, but they have to work quickly, and on top of each other. If that is not enough pressure, they have a television crew following their every move. **Thanks, Paul, Derek, Jason, Jose, Beata, Julia, Maryse, Jim, Peter, Jessica, and all your assistants and interns.** I'd like to thank Valorie Finnie for her immense talent and help with the vignettes in this book, Julie for dressing the sets, and George for photographing them.

There are two beautiful young women who are always by my side. Without them I would be lost. Dana MacKimmie has worked on every book, and there is not a photographed room or person she cannot find in a minute. Antonia Medeiros steers me from A to B with patience and a smile. **Thanks for your loyalty, Dana and Antonia.**

I have worked with my publisher, Clarkson Potter, for many years. They are simply the best. My editor Rosy Ngo's constant enthusiasm for this book and her clear guidance have kept us on the right track. Marysarah Quinn and Jan Derevjanik have taken my artistic visions and put them on the pages with great style. Jean Lynch and Joan Denman steered the book through the production process with an expert eye and meticulous attention to detail. **Thanks Rosy, Marysarah, Jan, Jean, and Joan.**

My life over the past ten years has been reinventing not only so many of your homes, but also working in front of a television camera. I would like to thank the many television channels around the globe that have allowed us to send our message of turning a house into a home to their viewers. My immense gratitude goes to the incredible enthusiasm and talent of everyone at Home and Garden Television in both the United States and Canada. **Thanks for the friendship and for supporting me in the best job in the world.**

contents

develop a **calm** mood >>   20

develop a **cheerful** mood >>   50

preface >> for the love of color

When I was twelve years old, my family bought our first color television. We were mesmerized by the programs that danced before us in full color. Today we don't give color television a second thought, but I still remember the joy of those early TV shows. That same pleasure is recaptured every time the first coats of paint are applied during my own television shows, *The Painted House* and *Debbie Travis' Facelift*. We have painted hundreds of rooms over the years, and every single one has evoked exciting responses from the whole team as those paint rollers sweep over the walls. Whether carpenters or sound technicians, we all have a sense of thrill and wonder as the dullest space is brought to life before our eyes.>> When it comes to our homes, we seem to have an innate fear of decorating with color. I know it's not true of everyone, but from my experience, and from the amount of beige, taupe, and builder's-white paint sold in the stores, there are many homeowners and renters out there who are scared to enliven their walls with a splash of color. A monochromatic house created around a palette of beige is fine, but it's your home, it's where you begin and end each day. This is where you raise your families and where memories are made. To me, "fine" is just not good enough, especially when it takes so little effort and cash to add color to your life with a coat of paint.>> This book was born out of my desire to share the stories and the excitement of working on the many *Facelift* shows where we have brought design and color into unsuspecting lives with ecstatic results. I am pleased to be able to share the tricks of my trade so that you can all experience the exhilaration of having a home that speaks to your heart.

introduction >>

This book is really two books in one. For *Facelift* fans, you will find some of your **favorite *Facelift* stories** about how we tackled various decorating problems. You will meet the marvelous families who took part in the shows. **We'll take a peek behind the scenes** and delve into the talents and personalities of the *Facelift* team. I have profiled them all, from Paul, Jason, and Derek, our talented and sexy carpenters, to Julia and Maryse, who style the rooms. You'll discover how this innovative team of carpenters, art director, painters, artists, and many more manage to pull together these designs in a matter of days, on a limited budget. Our work entails solving the problems of bad design or outdated décor, and creating something new and personal that the homeowner will adore. I will explain all the **whys and hows of each Facelift.**

The other part of this book is for every soul out there who is having difficulty choosing **a color palette** for his or her home. I have a simple trick that you can incorporate for successful results. The first question we *Facelift* team members ask ourselves when we begin the process of redesigning a space is not, What color do we paint this room? It's, **What mood do we intend the room to convey?** I will explain this philosophy and give examples of how you can produce your own mood with a particular solid color or color pattern. Then I'll show you how we use these techniques when we make over real-time homes for *Facelift*.

choose a mood . . . then choose a color . . .

Choosing a color story for your home can be maddeningly difficult. In these sections of the book I will explain how to make the process less stressful, and even enjoyable. There are armfuls of color books on the market. Many are beautiful coffee-table books filled with fields of lavender, Mediterranean colorwashed villas with shots of sun-drenched clay pots, and opulent gilded mansions. These books do a wonderful job of inspiring us to love color in all its glory, but how do we choose the correct color for our own walls? How do we translate these stunning pictures to our builder's-white suburban homes? When we design a room or an entire house on *Facelift,* we begin by deciding on the appropriate mood for the space. **In this book I am going to make you feel brave.** You will be armed with the knowledge and confidence to successfully personalize your space.>> The trick is to stop worrying about the color the walls should be, the furnishings you should pick, or the enormous array of possible fabrics. **Begin the decorating process by choosing a mood or even several moods for your home.** If you live in a small apartment, then the same tone or atmosphere may run throughout. A larger two- or three-story home could have several moods. Choose the mood by first deciding on how each room is used and by whom. Is the function of the space primarily for socializing or relaxing with your spouse? Are you a cheerful soul first thing in the morning? If so, then your bathroom should be filled with happy colors. Is your dining room a candlelit place to impress your friends with delicious food and stimulating conversation? Is there one space in the house that you can call your own—somewhere the mood is conducive to being quiet and calm? Are you looking for passion in the bedroom? >> **There are four positive moods that relate to the atmosphere of your home.** A **calm mood** is one that lowers your blood pressure, a Zen-like, serene space that invites you to relax. A **cheerful mood** is for a room conducive to happy chatter, a space that automatically makes you smile. Then there is a **nostalgic mood,** which is buoyed with treasured memories. This mood grounds us with a welcoming ambiance that makes us feel comfortable to be home. We all require a little drama in or lives. Here a **dramatic mood** displays our eclectic, even wild side. >> I have selected particular shades of colors and palettes that depict each mood. These will help with the style of furnishings and fabrics that will also complement the mood. I say shades or tones of color becase the same color can have many different moods. Let us consider yellow as an example. Pale, primrose yellow is relaxing; acid yellow is dramatic, even aggressive. A traditional golden yellow is always warm and inviting; a bright yellow will envelop a room in a sunny mood. >> When you have chosen the mood and the color, the next step is to decide how to trans- late that particular color into a wall pattern or texture. >> It is as simple as that. Decide on a mood, then on a color, and the rest will fall into place.

meet the facelift gang>>

debbie travis

People are always surprised when they learn that my background is not in design or decorating. In fact, I don't really have any architectural qualifications, unless you value an intense passion and enthusiasm for the home, all homes. I simply adore the whole journey. The almost voyeuristic process of selecting the *Facelift* homes always proves to be a riot, as we take intimate peeks into other families' lives. Then begins the challenge of designing rooms that will suit not only the homes but also the people inside them. What we try to do is make people's fantasies come to life, open their eyes to design ideas that they never even imagined, or would never attempt on their own. Once we're shooting the Facelift, I become the lady with the whip. We're on such a tight schedule that the whole team must keep moving, day and night. It's rather like a ballet as we all dance around one another's tasks with as much good humor as possible. We don't always hold our tempers in check, but we still leave every Facelift as friends. It's also a huge bonus when the person who was surprised with a new kitchen, bedroom, or entire house is left stunned but eternally thrilled with the whole episode. >> When not working, I am happiest surrounded by my own walls and my own family. I love cooking and just being around our kids. I also love to hike and have pounded the ground in many different countries. My decorating style ranges from wild and eclectic to sleek and modern, always with an infusion of nostalgia, and I have it all in my home. My motto is, "Why not!"

paul mcelligott, derek boudreau, and jason tustin

These three guys receive plenty of their own fan mail. I'm not sure if it's their amazing carpentry skills or their rugged good looks. >> **Paul** (center) is a perfectionist. The team has learned to avoid him when he is completely absorbed in a Facelift project. Although his work is intricate, it's his inventive skills that are unsurpassed. Paul dreams of one day building an open-concept home with a beautiful garden by a good beach. For now it's loft living with a strong South American flavor. >> **Derek** (right) is also a master craftsman. His favorite tool is a crowbar. He is always the first one in when we tear down walls. His tattoos have inspired several of our designs. Looking at Derek, it may seem strange that he prefers ultrapristine designs—clean, white, and anything French. >> **Jason** (left) is both a talented carpenter and a drummer. Better known for his hair and his love of music, his favorite color is what is found on his custom Ludwig drums—metallic orange. For his own decorating scheme, he thrives on recycling old pieces into funky-rustic designs. He likes to paint clean and natural, but not beige.

catherine pilon >>

Catherine is our director, the big boss, the one who gets to tell me what to do. On *Facelift* she spends her day staring at monitors, listening to chatter on the headphones, and talking that weird television language to her tech team. She is brilliant at seeing and hearing everything, and capturing the moments that make *Facelift* so special. She says that filming a reality show like *Facelift* is completely crazy, but fits with her past work making documentaries about rock stars and music videos. When not on set, Catherine loves movies, especially foreign films; listening to really loud music of all kinds in her car; snowboarding; and fashion. The true meaning of life for her is good food and good wine enjoyed in great company. Catherine's decorating style is a bit eclectic and wild, but cozy and warm. A room filled with light always makes her feel good.

16

scott bailey and travis champion>>

Scott (left) is a vital part of our gang. He began as a runner (someone on a television or movie set who literally runs errands for everyone). However, within weeks his amazingly amiable personality, his ability to make things happen, and his fast learning saw him promoted to assistant director. Without Scott I doubt we would ever finish the job on time. He loves the challenges of working in such demanding circumstances and expects a lot of himself and those around him. He describes his design style as modern and creative, but before he sets up the perfect home he is planning an extended trip to Australia to fulfill his passion for the surf. >> When **Travis** (right) is not listening to AC/DC, he is looking after everyone's needs on the set. As the equipment manager, he organizes the carpenters and painters and everyone else, and he takes the blame when things go wrong. (Well, except for the time Scott pushed me into the pool at Toby and DJ's farm—he loved that!) Travis' eye for design reflects his ear for rock 'n' roll. He feels most comfortable surrounded by nostalgic pieces from his music collections.

<< anne côté

Anne and I begin the process of every Facelift. We work first from our gut feelings about the space, then attempt to include the wishes of the homeowner from the information collected on the secret camera. As art director, Anne's personal approach to interior design is broad—she likes mostly bright colors in an earthy space. Her own home has a lipstick-red powder room. Her kitchen is a sleek mix of tangerine cabinets, steel countertops, a mirrored backsplash, and a chocolate cork floor. Her sense of adventure within the home also translates to the out-of-doors. She loves sailing, mountain climbing, and hiking, and her greatest wish is to design wild, public environments.

julia kininmonth and maryse rapsomatiotis >>

Julia (left) has the coolest job of all; she gets to go shopping for days. As set dresser, it's her role to put the finishing touches on the Facelifts, and the list is often long and eclectic—from sofas to throw cushions, mirrors, sinks, and flowers. Julia loves gossiping with her fellow *Facelift* mate Jim about their native Scotland. Julia's favorite design style steers toward dramatic colors and ethnic patterns and textures. Her many trips to India have inspired her love of Indian saris and teak furniture, along with beaded cushions in the deepest jewel tones. >> **Maryse** (right) first joined the team as a temporary intern from design school and then later, as assistant set dresser, she became a crucial complement to Julia's talents. At home, Maryse likes to keep things calm. Clean lines, sleek modern elements, and just a hint of funk keep her at peace in her own space. She has a quirky sense of humor, which helps her suffer her roommates' untidy lifestyle. >> Both Maryse and Julia's jobs seem glamorous, but the work also entails a huge amount of lugging furniture and rolls of carpets, bringing several choices of everything to the homes, and then returning all the unused pieces.

<< jose brady and beata nawrocki

Jose (right) is our volatile head painter. Beware anyone who steps near his wet walls because he takes immense pride in his work. His biggest nightmare on set, and rightly so, was when he painted latex over oil, and the walls had to be completely stripped. His favorite tools are his specialty paintbrushes and Beata. Jose is so tall that he rarely

needs a ladder. In his own home he chooses to keep things subtle and simple, with blacks, grays, and stone finishes, and prefers 12-foot ceilings.>> Always an artist at heart, **Beata** (left) loves bold color and incorporating original photography into her decorating style. She is a native of Poland and works tirelessly on the set, with a great sense of humor that is always appreciated. She loves red, and lives surrounded by a jumble of prewar furnishings, paintings, photography, and work areas. Beata dreams of a spacious country house surrounded by trees, and if there were ever time between Facelifts, she would like to write.

jim connelly and peter de sousa >>

Jim's (right) sparkling Scottish wit is responsible for the high spirits during the makeovers, however stressful they may be. I have been known to drive him quite mad with my impatient requests for magical paint finishes that must be done super-humanly in a very short time frame. But his work is always imaginative and executed brilliantly. Jim's favorite color is black, as it looks good with his white hair, of which he is very proud. At home Jim fancies Old World, European style: the formal château look, with burnished moldings, glowing textured patinas on walls and furniture, and decadent, tactile fabrics. >> **Peter** (left) is a master at paint and plaster finishes, and works quietly and meticulously to get the job done no matter what's going on around him. His favorite *Facelift* episode is the plantation bedroom (page 89), which is odd because his task was not plastering a special finish, but hanging expensive wallpaper, and this was his first time at the job. Peter's chosen home décor is French Country; the comforting ambiance of distressed wood floors and cabinets and toile fabrics make him happy.

<< jessica rodriguez

As production assistant, Jessica drives around collecting supplies for the show, so perhaps it's understandable that she adores the cube truck. In fact, she thinks of it as her second home. She likes to be busy, plays baseball with a vengeance, and wants her own home. Jessica's background in interior design has swayed her preferences to clean, modern arrangements and baby blue.

the tech team>>

It is rare that the technical side of television is ever seen, but *Facelift* is a true reality show and these guys follow all the action with their cameras. The talent required for this job includes not only excellent skills with a lens and a mike but also the ability to run very fast whenever and wherever needed. Alongside the constant renovation, the dramas happen with rapid fire. Erick, Barry, and Ray are there with their big heavy cameras capturing the goings-on. Petro has a smaller, less intimidating camera and he manages to film the stickier, more emotional moments. The grips, or lighting experts, Hugo and Alexis, make sure that the room, the team, and yours truly look their very best. Johnny is responsible for allowing us to hear what goes on, even when surrounded by the intense noise of the renovation and the constant stream of chatting and laughing. Mimi, our makeup artist, has the toughest job—making me look decent no matter what's going on.

FROM LEFT TO RIGHT Mireille "Mimi" St-Laurent, Erick St-Hilaire, Debbie Travis, Jean "Johnny" Asselin, Petro Duszara, Catherine Pilon, and Hugo Roy. NOT SHOWN Alexis Marcoux, Barry Russell, and Ray Quenneville.

develop a

calm mood

choose a calm mood . . . Imagine yourself walking into a room and immediately feeling relaxed. Lay your head against the softest cushion, run your bare toes through a silky rug, sink back into a hot, foam-filled bath, and experience the fading of the tensions of the day. This is the calming mood for a home or particular room that is a refuge from the stress of the daily grind. It's an environment that gently recharges your battery. The ambiance is tranquil and serene. >> There are many reasons to imbue a room of your own with a calming mood. Perhaps you are looking for the perfect place to meditate, a quiet space in which to empty the mind. You may want a living room where

you can kick off your shoes and sink into the deepest sofa, or a place to eat in a peaceful, even romantic setting; a bathroom to begin your day in a contemplative state, or a bedroom that invites you to wind down and sleep with ease. >> If this is the mood you wish to create, then you must strive for balance. These Zen-like spaces are utterly simple, lacking in clutter and any element of busyness. They are designed around colors, textures, and shapes that lead both the mind and body into the whole sensual experience.

BELOW Splashes of turquoise punctuate the surrounding earthy tones, while a few well-chosen objects arranged in varying heights are all that are needed to finish the room. LEFT An inexpensive side table painted pale blue is the perfect foil for the plain steel lamp and white paper shade. PRECEDING PAGES, LEFT The shadow-block pattern on the wall, achieved by painting a golden metallic glaze over alternate squares, produces many shades and shapes from dark and loamy to tarnished gold. PRECEDING PAGES, RIGHT Pale sky blue is an important Zen color, reminding us of peace and open spaces. The suede cushion has been detailed with a silk Japanese obi sash that shimmers and reflects.

. . . choose a calm color

Colors that soothe the senses are those found in the **neutral or natural spectrum.** Because of their association with nature they evoke an immediate sense of **purity** and **serenity.** The range of these harmonious colors is as vast as the outside world from which they come: the **earth, sea, and sky.**

Browns, taupes, creams, and all tones of white are favorite choices for peaceful settings. The selection is immense and clearly associated with the senses. Think of the silky, succulent taste of chocolate, the many tactile tones of wood, a first snowfall, or the color of sand. The mood of a room painted in these naturals can turn either cooler or warmer depending on what colors and textures sit alongside them. Tones of gray provide a note of contrast by cooling down the warm, creamy walls (see Nadia's den on page 45). Stone and sand colors can be enlivened with contrasting colors such as a splash of baby blue.

Earthy greens, commonly used in places of study such as libraries and schools, are regenerative and soothing. The palest milky greens combined with other neutral colors will produce a quiet room. Imagine dove-gray painted floors

BELOW Lavender dining room walls invite quiet talk and perhaps a contemplative mood. An off-white cork floor adds an unassuming and harmonious accent note that completes the serene setting. A wooden runner, fiber placemats, sushi trays, and a delicate arrangement of wild grasses in a textured ceramic vase work in unison to bring the room to life. RIGHT The mix of colors and patterns on the table, the delicate Asian floral on the frosted glass, and the cross-weave fiber and dark brown reed mats create a peaceful balance, as they do in nature.

with the subtlest moss-green walls; the effect is almost spiritual. Think of a walk in the country on a summer's day and how this world of green immediately calms you and improves your mood. Used in large spaces, rich dark greens will anchor a room, but to remain restful these greens should be **balanced** with plenty of natural woods and off-whites.

The right mix of colors will always create an oasis of calm.

Blue is synonymous with the sea and the sky, but there are many hues. The cooler blues, from slate gray to the palest duck-egg blue, are receding colors and will provide the feeling of openness and space. Lilacs and lavenders, blues with the slightest hint of red, will evoke calm and tranquility. Watery blues in a bathroom are heavenly, and are ideally mixed with an abundance of white for a sense of purity and serenity.

The simplicity **of white** and its many tints, from the bluish hue of milk white to the deepest beige linen, all have a sensuous beauty. However, white can be harsh, as often seen throughout the minimalist period of

design. Balance is key to keeping white walls harmonious with their surroundings. Splashes of color, seen in Elsy's home on page 39, can add simply to the soothing ambiance of the off-white walls and furnishings. In Sigal's den on page 33, the purity of the white wall works well with a combination of aged white brick and wine-colored cork floors.

All whites have a mysterious quality because of their ability to constantly change with the light. The serene mood is enhanced by the surrounding colors inside and outside the home. The effect of the reflection of trees on an interior white wall is as sublime as is the purplish glow from a recent snowfall.

The right mix of colors will always create an oasis of calm, but **textures and shapes** also play a vital part in a

ABOVE LEFT Calming walls have been made more important with the lavish touch of silver leaf. The reflective quality of the leaf continues onto the table with stainless steel cutlery and accessories. Candlelight enhances the mirrored characteristics of the silver as well as the glassware, creating an enchanting place that beckons you and a friend to share a quiet, special meal. ABOVE RIGHT It is in the pairing of opposites that we find a restful and harmonious state. Here, the two-tone effect in both color and sheen is captured in the mix of flat mauve mats on a shiny table, slate-gray plates with silver napkin rings, and a pristine white linen napkin.

serene space. Patinas on wall surfaces are one of the easiest and least expensive methods of highlighting a mood. A **metallic wash** applied to alternate squares on the living room walls, as on page 20, is luxurious, reflective, and soothing.

Patterns on walls or in fabrics should be kept simple to create a calm and serene mood, but they can be both **free-flowing** or geometric and still enhance the restful ambiance. **Texture is visual and tactile.** Once again, balance is just as important with the use of texture as it is with color, but not necessarily equal balance. Hard textures are generally installed at the base of the room, such as hardwood floors, and they live with the soft textures found in fabrics and furnishings.

A Zen-like neutral space can work in beautiful harmony with an endless combination of materials. Bare wood, stone, cork, and tile floors all have unique natural textures and can be softened with the quirky touch of a sisal or shag rug. Furnishings, fixtures, and fittings should have a sense of fluidity. **Natural fibers** should be used

BELOW This bedroom is alive with soothing textures. Both the wooden plate and vine balls are beautiful renditions of common elements, while the bed linens are visibly soft and smooth. A raised shelf set asymmetrically above the bed replaces the headboard, and the uncomplicated arrangement of colors and objects is restful and assuring. RIGHT A special pattern or texture found in a single object, such as the intricate circles in this wooden plate, makes a restful focal point.

ABOVE The clean blue of the pillow and thin blue lines on the wall pop the neutral colors and keep the room fresh as well as harmonious and relaxing. There is a peaceful juxtaposition, of woven-fabric headboard and braided-fiber side table set against the smooth cotton duvet and walls, that invites quiet repose and snuggling between the sheets. Creamy-beige sheers are warm and soothing in the evening, yet allow daylight to flood the room. LEFT The textured weave of the fabric headboard highlights a myriad of natural wood and sky-blue shades that are picked up on the walls and bed linens.

wherever possible to allow the body to breathe. Something as simple as a favorite object alone on a table or shelf can evoke a feeling of peace. A smooth ceramic bowl, a small group of pebbles or seashells, or a grouping of interesting glass bottles will rest the eyes.

If you are now inspired to create your own space with a calm and serene mood, then turn the page and enjoy the following Facelifts.

OPPOSITE, TOP Pale aqua walls and creamy-white wood present subtle hints of color to the stark white porcelain and stone floor. Simple, unfettered design elements and the use of natural fibers in the wooden mat contribute to a pure, spalike mood. OPPOSITE, BOTTOM Details of color and texture arouse the senses, particularly in a bathroom where we are alone and open to quiet contemplation. A clear glass shelf floats against a sea of pale aqua, while the contrast in textures of the rippled vase and floral soap invite your touch.

RIGHT Painted bamboo stalks float across the upper walls, adding an Asian-inspired vitality to the room's peaceful mood. BELOW Alternating sheens and textures—semigloss paint for the wainscoting, a light stone floor, and a fluffy bath mat bring balance. Raffia storage boxes are an easy way to liven up a space with natural materials. BELOW RIGHT The sinuous shape of a box that has been lovingly formed and polished speaks softly but makes a big impact on the daily bath ritual. Start and end with an image that speaks to your spirit.

Balance is key to keeping white walls harmonious with their surroundings.

pure white facelift >>

Good friends are a gift; best friends are a luxury. This is the story of how a couple of lifelong buddies came to the aid of their best friend, who longed for a Facelift. Susan, Jody, and Sigal met in the eighth grade. Over the next twenty or so years their lives were intertwined with boyfriends, followed by weddings and the inevitable riches of family life, babies, and homes. Sigal and her husband, Mitchell, had hit hard times, so renovating and decorating their suburban house had been pushed aside. Sigal, Mitchell, and their twin seven-year-old daughters spend a lot of time in the family den. Sigal adores her family but loathes this den; her friends hate the den and adore Sigal. Me, well, it seemed like a recipe for success.

after > >

before > >

the challenge >> The den measured about 18 feet by 14 feet but appeared poky with the 1970s décor. Yellowing wood-paneled walls plus a worn-out parquet floor dominated the cavelike space. The beamed ceiling was also an issue, drawing attention to poorly made box beams. As in most family rooms, the television dominated the space. My challenge was to keep the TV but hide it.

<< antiqued **brick wall**

To create a unified focal point in Sigal's den, I put up faux-brick panels on either side of the brick fireplace. I then smeared plaster randomly over the panels so that some areas of the faux brick were covered, but the brick shape could still be seen in other areas. The whole wall was primed, painted white, and glazed to highlight the rough texture. You can purchase fake brick panels in 4- by 8-foot sheets at your lumber or hardware store.

INSTRUCTIONS

step 1. Apply a thin coat of plaster to the faux brick in random sections, leaving some of the fake brick bare. Using a spatula or trowel and the cross-hatch technique, spread the plaster.

step 2. To highlight the rough edges of the plaster, mix a creamy-yellow-colored glaze, equal parts paint and glaze. Brush on the glaze and rub it with a rag, making sure to get into all the creases and crevices of the plaster.

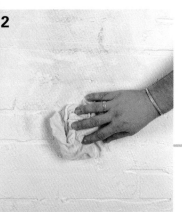

the facelift >> Over four days we completely changed this dingy den into a bright California-style haven. According to her conspiring friends, Sigal felt that an all-white room would make the den look larger. I agreed to a point, but not all white. The plan for a **light airy** den was perfect, but it needed grounding with a dramatic dark floor. While Jose sanded the sugar-icing peaks off the ceiling's stucco finish, Derek and Paul transformed the ceiling by making a series of identical beams and fitting them together with the existing beams in an **eye-catching grid of oversized squares.** As a finishing touch, a subtle embossed design was stenciled into the corners of the squares using plaster instead of paint, and the whole ceiling was painted flat white.

Now when one enters the den, the eye is drawn to the fireplace. Instead of diminishing the brick fireplace, we added to it. Sheets of fake-brick paneling were installed and the whole surface was then treated to look like an **old plastered white** wall.

Sigal's furniture had seen better days, so it was shamelessly relegated to the basement and replaced with a **powder-blue sofa,** which is glorious with the dark, Bordeaux-colored floating cork floor, which was laid to give substance to this all-white room. Tiny boxes were attached to the

white fireplace wall to play on scale. These we used for candles, but they could also hold miniature objects. The whole process of designing Sigal's den was about the concept of space. A small area needs to be allowed to breathe. We lost the clutter, lightened the walls, added detail to the ceiling, and firmly established the room with the rich dark floors.

building a mood with color >> While an all-white room conjures up images of **purity** and **tranquility,** the mood is enhanced greatly by pairing the monotone palette with the deep wine tones of the cork floor. The white plastered brick fireplace wall is made more **restful** with a light umber glaze, and gray paint strokes transform the panels.

<< embossed-tin **armoire**

The television is not a great-looking focal point on its own, so we hid it away in a beautiful armoire, which was decorated to enhance Sigal's serene, all-white family room. I transformed a store-bought cabinet with sheets of pressed tin and white paint, stained to look antique. The doors were reframed and rehinged so that they would open up flat against the sides of the armoire.

INSTRUCTIONS

For best results, prepare your surface following the preparation tips on page 139.

step 1. Remove the doors and place them on a flat work surface.

step 2. Cut a sheet of pressed tin to size, and nail and glue it into position on the front of the door.

step 3. Nail on wood trim to cover the edges of the tin and make a frame.

step 4. Using metal primer for the tin, prime and paint the doors and the rest of the armoire white.

step 5. Dip tea bags in water and rub them over the surface of the armoire, including the pressed tin, to highlight the pattern and age the fresh paint.

step 6. Apply 2 coats of varnish to protect the finish.

harmonious facelift >>

This is a love story, and love can be painfully complicated. Felipe and Elsy, both from large South American families, had been dating for years. They're both in their midtwenties now, and they wanted to marry, but something was holding them back. Felipe had inherited his beloved grandmother's house  and made it his home. He adored this 1960s bungalow just the way it was. The décor, however, made Elsy run for cover. Small rooms with walls covered in dingy floral wallpaper, green shag carpeting, and Granny's odd bits of furniture did nothing for their romance. They were at a stalemate, and that's when I received Felipe's desperate letter. There was a delicious twist to the story. If we would help him redecorate the house so that Elsy felt at home, Felipe could propose to her.

after >>

before >>

demolition tips

ask a professional

Before breaking down a wall, as we did in Elsy's living room, you **must** ensure that the wall is not load bearing. If it is part of the building's structure, the floor above will sag and eventually collapse. Load-bearing walls can be removed, but temporary supports must be built until the wall is down, and then an I-beam must be installed across the new opening. Walls hide electrical wiring, plumbing pipes, and heat vents. Take care that these are not damaged and that they are rerouted safely. Always use a licensed electrician and plumber.

safety first

Along with the satisfaction of smashing through drywall and/or plaster comes the risk of flying debris, dirt, and great clouds of dust. Protect yourself with safety goggles, a mask, and work gloves. If working above your head, wear a hard hat. Remove children and animals from the site.

Protect the floor with a drop cloth, and be aware that the dust will travel through to other rooms. Seal door openings with sheets of plastic and tape, and cover all furniture with drop cloths or old sheets.

hard-hitting tools

Rent or buy proper tools for the job: a sledgehammer; a heavy, short-handled hammer; a stone chisel for taking off jutting brick; and a reciprocating saw for cutting through lath, studs, and metal.

recycle and reuse

What comes down doesn't necessarily all go to the scrap heap. Wood and metal sheeting can be reused in other projects. Old boards make great rustic furniture.

the challenge >> Elsy was right. The house was in a depressing state, and because the *Facelift* team are great romantics, we rose to the challenge. The idea was to inject some youthful energy and **blissful colors** into the décor. We would completely **modernize** the ground floor by losing the original decorations and reconfiguring the walls. I wanted to **open up** the whole ground floor so that you walked from the vestibule into the living and dining areas. We also planned to close off the original tiny kitchen, which opened into the dining room, building a new wall. But to keep the kitchen from appearing too small, we designed a pass-through window, reminiscent of the '60s and once again back in vogue.

the facelift >> During five incredibly crazy days, the wall between the living room and dining room was removed and a new wall was built to hide the kitchen. All the original kitchen cabinets were painted, the lower ones in a **contemporary** shade of tangerine. The avocado stove went out, and a white stove and refrigerator moved in. Once the grimy carpet was removed, we found hardwood floors. They were scuffed and worn, so a couple of evenings were spent sanding and priming, and then two coats of **bright** white floor paint were applied. The old floor tiles in the kitchen were scraped up, and fresh light gray and white vinyl tiles were laid in both the kitchen and dining areas.

The palest primrose yellow was used on the walls throughout, and immediately we had a new, sunny space. We now had light streaming in through the two large windows draped in **airy** white sheers. Granny's furnishings were stored in Felipe's basement, and a combination of built-in benches and shelves along with new, sleek-lined pieces finished the **youthful** transformation.

building a mood with color >> Budget-conscious but brilliant design and color played a key role in setting the **serene, modern** mood. Soft, butter-yellow walls cast a warm hue over the **unfettered** surroundings, while white floors throughout expand and unify the open space. A few hot color accents lift the calming spirit of the pale background. Tangerine kitchen cupboards and red and citrus-green cushions are contemporary and fun. The overall picture is **harmonious** and **peaceful.**

restful facelift >>

Nadia's **dream** was to live in a converted city **loft** with today's **calming, Zen**-inspired colors. This mood of tranquility was the complete opposite of the exuberant surroundings she was used to. She and her husband, Angelo, had been brought up in the same traditional, tightly knit neighborhood, and they both wanted to stay around their friends and large Italian families. Nadia's **lofty** ideas, however, came down to earth when she and Angelo moved into a small duplex around the corner from both their parents. Angelo's job was the basement, and he hadn't a clue where to start. We decided to offer Angelo and this young marriage a helping hand by giving their basement a thoroughly modern **Facelift.**

before >>

after >>

the challenge >> The basement was right out of a '70s movie set—dark, heavy, cluttered, and a bit overdramatic. It came equipped with the classic parquet flooring, pine-paneled walls, a brick fireplace, and Spanish-style brick shelving. It even had the quintessential drinks bar. Our challenge was to infuse this space with a **light, tranquil** ambiance that encouraged easy **breathing** and **restful** pursuits.

the facelift >> The plan was to give Nadia the feel of the **open loft space** she had always wanted. With the help of Angelo's brothers, we spent the first day demolishing the brick walls and tearing out the stair railing. We replaced heavy, textured materials with **streamlined** walls. During the night, we built a wall that would separate the stairs from the room and allow for a new sofa beside it.

During the second day, the wood paneling was covered with drywall. To give the fireplace a **contemporary** look, we changed the shape by building up the edges with plywood and covering the brick with rough plaster. We made a sleek, glossy white double coffee table out of hollow-core doors. A shape was cut and the open part filled in with trim.

The last days were spent replacing the Spanish-style shelving with a **modern, open** system of simple, ready-made cubes. These were glamorized by inserting mirrored tile at the back of each cube. The parquet floor was sanded and then painted a low-sheen charcoal gray. A large, checkered pattern was produced by applying high-gloss varnish to alternate large squares. We chose **tactile** textures—silky leather sofas and a deep-pile shag rug, which are both **soothing** and **inviting.**

<< varnish shadow blocks

Painted floors can be as naïve or sophisticated as you please. I wanted to update the old parquet floor to match the young, modern mood we were creating in Nadia's basement Facelift. I painted it with dark gray, low-sheen floor paint, then marked off a grid of squares (made easy by following the original parquet lines). Alternate squares were taped off and painted with oil-based, high-gloss varnish.

building a mood with color >> This basement room was virtually windowless and had a low ceiling. Both color and sheen worked their magic to produce the **light, spacious** mood that Nadia craved. We went with a purely **neutral** palette. The walls and ceiling are a buttery cream, but we stepped up the sheen from satin to gloss on the ceiling, as the **reflective** quality gives the impression of height. The charcoal gray shadow squares designed around the old parquet floor ground the room and give it a modern architectural edge.

dreamy facelift >>

Robert was thrilled by the numerous surprise birthday and anniversary parties his wife, Shelley, had arranged, but he had never been able to return the favor. After watching an episode of *Facelift,* he saw an opportunity "to get her back." The plain white walls and shabby furnishings in their dull master bedroom went unnoticed by Robert, but Shelley's disdain was definitely noted. Robert was as eager as a small boy with a firecracker not only to surprise his wife with a new bedroom but also to have the opportunity to orchestrate the entire process. He was a delight to work with, my kind of sneaky guy.

before > >

< < after

the challenge >> Our bedrooms deserve to be given special attention because we spend so much time in them. They are indeed sanctuaries. Shelley and Robert's room, on the other hand, was uninspiring. It could be described as little more than a plain white box. Venetian blinds, worn and dated; wall-to-wall carpet; and unattractive bed linens will do little to inspire us. It all had to go.

the facelift >> While Shelley was away, the *Facelift* team had three days to

convert the bedroom into a sensual sleeping den. Robert looked on gleefully with their thirteen-year-old daughter, Cayla, as we removed everything and gave this bedroom some personality. I decided on modern wood panels, instead of painted walls, that would wrap the room in an **uncluttered** shell. The walls were 8 feet tall, which is the standard length of plywood panels. Birch plywood was chosen for its superior grain, and each panel was attached from floor to ceiling with wood adhesive and nails. The seams along each panel and around the ceiling and floor were covered with strips of 1- by 2-foot pine. All the plywood and pine pieces were stained deep chestnut brown and varnished in a midsheen before being applied to the walls. The many doors in the bedroom would have detracted from the rich flow of the dark paneling, so we covered them with birch veneer stained to match.

venetian plaster fireplace

To give the electric fireplace more presence, I built a plywood surround and decorated it to look like stone. I used Venetian plaster, which is silky smooth and can be burnished to a high sheen. We applied a thin coat of plaster to the primed plywood with a trowel, then went over it with cross-hatch strokes to get a smooth finish. The dry plaster was lightly sanded to get rid of any ridges or rough edges. A khaki-colored glaze was mixed, 1 part paint to 3 parts glazing liquid, and rubbed over the plaster to produce the shading of stone. To seal and protect the work, 2 coats of matte varnish were applied.

Since I was aiming for **pure comfort,** the next element was a fireplace. With no existing chimney, we opted for an electric fire and built a plywood surround. The mantel was finished with a length of dark stained wood, and the front and sides were roughly coated in tinted plaster. The bed was moved in front of the window, which was unconventional but necessary because the fireplace had taken up the bed wall. **Luxurious** silk drapes line the wall behind the custom headboard we made from old pine stained the deepest honey. The palest blue painted ceiling completes this **harmonious** bedroom.

building a mood with color >>

What we wanted to convey in Shelley and Robert's bedroom was a feeling of **serenity** that was both **sumptuous** and **cozy.** The dark teak-stained paneling resonates with warmth, and yet the lines of the paneling and headboard are **simple** and **modern.** Blue and champagne-beige satin sheets and silk curtains are colors and materials that are **soothing** and **seductive** at the same time. There is nothing to interrupt the sexy ambiance of this grown-up bedroom.

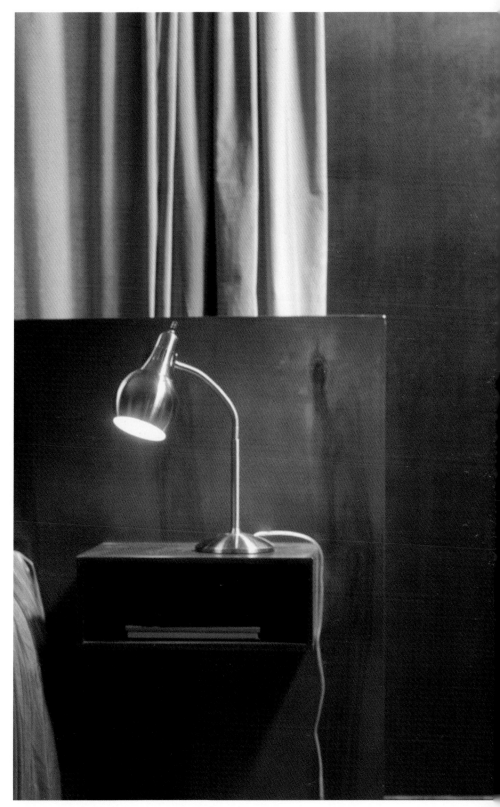

develop a

cheerful
mood

choose a cheerful mood . . .

Some spaces make you smile on entering, immediately uplifting your mood. These are happy rooms. Of course, the presence of a big family, little ones at bath time, a noisy dinner table, or a child's bedroom filled with toys can be vital elements. We all hope our dinner parties will be lively affairs with the help of good food, wine, and vivacious company, but how important is the décor? Well, you will need some of everything, but the expressive use of color and pattern can take you far. >> If you wish to noticeably perk up when you walk into a room, then choose a cheerful mood. Children's rooms should always be joyful places, and lessons can be learned here for the rest of us. If early mornings are not your most resounding time of day, then possibly your bedroom and bathroom need that lift to put a spring in your step. We would all love to look radiant in the bedroom, or anywhere, for that matter. With reflective colors on the wall, even the palest skin will have a healthy hue. Bright colors have been growing in popularity, possibly since the abundance of the beige-on-beige interiors in the '90s, but nowhere is this trend more prevalent than in the kitchen. Even the common kitchen utensil has become a piece of lively, colorful art. Appliances are gradually becoming acceptable in a rainbow of choices, and picking cabinets is a far cry from just wood veneers or white laminate. A cheerful mood in the home is about enjoying the laughter of your children, the warmth of coffee with a friend, and raising your spirits even on the dullest day.

... choose a cheerful color

Happiness is connected to energy, and without one, we don't have the other. In the same way as with a warm and alive color, a **happy** mood vibrates with energy. The mood of a dismal north-facing room is automatically **brightened** with a fresh coat of yellow paint. A dark oak kitchen can be inexpensively **perked** up with apple-green walls. The most obvious example of a dreary and depressing interior trend is the dreaded wood-paneled basement, of which I have revamped more than my fair share (see Karen's basement on page 68). Just the initial coat of primer will immediately change the ambiance of these low-energy rooms. In order to bring a **vibrant** mood into a particular space, we must first lose our reserve, then have **fun** and abandon with our color choice.

Yellow and orange are the colors most closely associated with lifting our **spirits**. The wide range of hues radiates different levels of emotions. A pale yellow bathroom can gently wake us with a smile in the morning. Radiant yellows are as optimistic and glorious as the sun itself and **stimulating** for both children and adults. A warm yellow brings sunshine into a cold playroom and simultaneously enhances creative play. But caution is always advised with this color. The shade you pick

ABOVE The cool brushed metals, glass, and plastic materials are livened up by the invigorating turquoise walls, while the cork floor is a warm, grounding element. Black and white together (the framed picture) or black alone (the chairs) bring out the best in their surroundings by punctuating the color. LEFT Orange is always a mood lifter, friendly and warm, adding the perfect accent to this modern combination.

PRECEDING PAGES, LEFT Applied on the wall with a stencil, this pattern is reminiscent of the lively fabrics from the vivacious '50s. Water colors are both soothing and vibrant, and balance the cool metal table. PRECEDING PAGES, RIGHT No fuss, no muss, just simple, fresh breakfast fare delivered in a bright, modern setting. Orange and blue are both retro and contemporary, and always uplifting.

may not have the **impact** intended. Although a social color, vivid yellow can bring out the argumentative side in us. Its boldness can clash with a guest's ego, so think carefully before putting a **bright** sunny yellow in a dining room. Yellow can also be cool.

Happiness is connected to energy, and without one,

There is little warmth in lemons; these citrus yellows are better saved for dramatic spaces (see the dramatic dining room on page 115). Softer shades will always be welcoming and **joyful** when balanced with plenty of white for the freshest mood. Tone down the brightest yellows with accents of gray blues.

Orange, although more bold than yellow, is easier on the eye. A flaming orange dining room is captivating and full of celebration, probably the most sociable of all colors. Orange visually advances toward us, making a room feel cozier and smaller. This welcoming mood is perfect for kitchens (see Emma's on page 74), living rooms, and accent walls in large loft spaces, but I would leave its outgoing personality out of the bedroom or study area. The **lively** mood of orange ranges from

we don't have the other.

deep terra-cotta, apricot, and the colors found in the most succulent peach. If the intensity of orange walls carries too much **vitality** for your home, then use its **liveliness** as accents to warm up cooler colors.

Pinks can be both dramatic and **fun**, with a great sense of movement and **sparkle**—ask any seven-year-old girl. Rosy pinks imply that we have an **optimistic** view of life. A peach-pink

LEFT Crisp white wainscoting grounds these lively walls and lets them dominate. The dark textured towels and robe add luxurious color and depth. ABOVE Children will love these busy bubbles stenciled on in muted tones of yellow and green.

OPPOSITE, BOTTOM Butter yellow is a feel-good color that stimulates gently. The marine-blue mirror frame and shelf underline the simplicity of the basic elements, as does the single flower on the sink. The cheerful floor mat provides a nice burst of energy. OPPOSITE, TOP Multistriped towels are full of life; yellow, blue, and white pull all the colors of the bathroom together.

whimsical

playful

charming

dining room is both friendly and flattering. Pink can be just as **inviting** on a floor as on the walls, as seen in Karen's basement on page 71. Add a touch of blue to pink, and a variety of warm lilacs and lavenders is produced. Too much blue, and the mood cools into mauves and purples.

Blues are traditionally associated with a calm mood, but once combined with a little green, they lose their meditative quality. These refreshing turquoises and aquas are youthful and **invigorating**. Reflective of the feelings experienced as we move through water, these colors imbue pure clarity with a relaxed energy. Blue-greens are receding colors that open up spaces, making them appear bigger. Turquoise is one of the few hues that is both **vibrant** and soothing. It makes an ideal choice for bathrooms—calming yet compelling—and will sit happily alongside the brightest yellows, blues, or greens.

Greens can be peaceful or nostalgic, and there are certain tints of green that will always make us smile. Think of a young bud just before it opens fully.

ABOVE New-leaf green is young and bold, paired with the always optimistic pink. This is a space for giggling children and family fun. LEFT The satin glaze on the vase highlights its smooth curves and joyous bubblegum color.

OPPOSITE Stripes introduce a note of sophistication, but their ragged shape is whimsical. Nothing is too precious or serious. FAR LEFT The wall colors may seem wild, but nature has always loved them.

This is an endearing and cheerful palette; lavender and lilac are youthful shades

On the fun side that swings toward dramatic, there are tangy limes and wild acid greens. These greens are **exciting** and full of life. Lime green as an accessory will be that spark in a more neutral setting. Green and white in a bedroom will be as fresh and **inviting** as it is relaxing. Accented with bright pink (see the living room on page 57), a sharp fresh yellow-green makes me want to bounce a giggling baby on my knee.

Bright colors are often for the brave at heart; start by taking a few small steps with brightly colored cushions and fabrics, vases, frames, and bowls. Keep furnishings uncluttered and clean lined so they don't fight with that vibrant color scheme.

OPPOSITE Floating lines of stenciled flowers dominate the room, signaling an optimistic and vigorous mood. The simple linear design theme is picked up by the thin-stripe pillowcases.

RIGHT Deep pink and green against the lavender walls is a modern combination that makes it hard not to smile. The flowers are stenciled on at a fraction of the cost of wallpaper.

made more **pronounced** by the white trim.

cheerful facelifts >>>>>

sunny facelift >>>

I have been lucky to encounter numerous special individuals in my life, but the time I spent with Reverend Gray was a privilege. He is from South Carolina and is the epitome of southern charm. When we first met, he talked lovingly about his wife and four daughters and their small church-owned home. As much as Olive adores cooking for her family, she found no enjoyment working in the blandness of her kitchen. The couple had discussed the problem, but there were no extra pennies from the reverend's church salary to be spent on décor. That's where I came in.

before >>

< < before

after > >

<< garden **armoire**

I put an old china cabinet to work as a much-needed cupboard to hold garden pots and accessories. I took inspiration from the homeowner's love of plants and bright colors, and glued huge flowers to the doors, inside and out. These oversized blossoms keep the promise of spring blooming all year round. For best results, prepare your surface following the preparation tips on page 139.

step 1. Paint 2 coats of a semigloss white base coat, and let the paint dry for 4 hours.

step 2. Blow up large colored prints of bright flowers.

step 3. Using sharp scissors, cut carefully around the prints.

step 4. To keep the colors from running, spray varnish the cutouts.

step 5. Brush decoupage glue over the front and back of the cutouts and stick them into position on the cabinet. Press down firmly with a paper roller to force out any air bubbles.

step 6. Apply 2 coats of varnish to protect your finish.

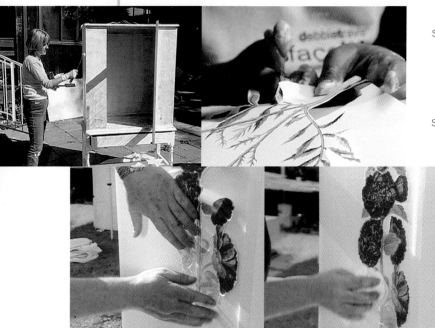

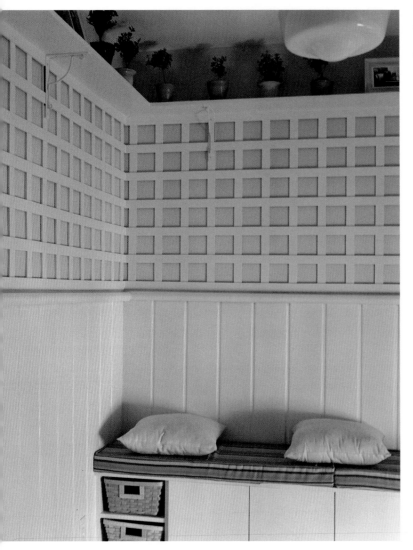

the challenge >> The Grays' home had few frills. The kitchen was actually three small rooms; the cooking area was compact, with an eating room off it that led into a sunroom that was used primarily for plants. Olive has a passion for plants, but this space lacked inspiration for her green thumb. The appliances had seen happier days, the painted cabinets were in good condition but dull, the fake-wood countertops were peeling badly in places, and the tile floors were cracked. The walls in all the rooms were a hideous mixture of peeling paint, wood paneling, and vintage '70s tile. We had our work cut out for us.

the facelift >> When you have only four days to transform a kitchen, the first task is to be brutally honest about what you can achieve in such a short period of time. We decided to remove the arches from around the kitchen window and the entrance onto the sunroom. This would open up all three spaces and incorporate flow into the otherwise chopped-up area. We laid down a floating linoleum floor in two colors straight over the old linoleum in the kitchen area and the parquet in the sunroom. The green and beige planks were cut into sizes that, when clicked into place, created huge diamond shapes.

Next came the painting. The wood paneling was painted the palest yellow and the walls were done in **sunny** green. The cabinets

custom seating >>

Built-in furniture and storage are efficient ways to optimize on space. The wall of benches in Olive's small, garden-style breakfast room allows for much-needed extra seating as well as storage below. Brightly upholstered cushions and pillows add color and comfort.

were sanded smooth and then painted a **luminous** green. Panels were cut out of the top cupboard doors with a jigsaw and replaced with etched glass including words associated with southern cooking. These glass inserts immediately updated and **brightened** the kitchen. The eating area of the kitchen was dressed up to complement the sunny feeling of the sunroom. We made a lattice with 1-inch strips of painted pine over a green base. The effect was inexpensive and simple to achieve, and now meals can

be enjoyed within the ambiance of a **charming**, sunny terrace. To extend the illusion, I took the liberty of reinventing a cabinet where Olive kept extra plates.

building a mood with color >> Warm and **cheerful** shades of green and yellow, along with the fresh, clean subway tiles, are all the elements required to make this an inviting place for **happy** family meals.

perky pink facelift >>>

Karen has three daughters whom she has brought up alone since the tragic death of their father two years ago. Carly, twenty-one; Ali, seventeen; and Lauren, the baby of the family at thirteen, have been the guiding light and staunch support behind Mom during tough times. When they wrote to us explaining that they were desperate to put some **color and zing** back into their mom's life, the *Facelift* team jumped at the opportunity. The process was far more difficult and emotional than we could possibly have envisioned.

before >>

<< after

after > >

the challenge >> The plan was to give them a family room where they could hang out together. Like so many homes, the basement was being used to store everything from countless school projects to old rabbit cages and discarded furniture. This floor-to-ceiling chaos was discouraging enough, but there was a far more fundamental dilemma: the basement was also packed with their father's belongings. It took a bunch of strangers to unravel the turmoil. Everything else was put into piles of either "trash," "keep," or "give away." After one long and dirty day, we had an empty basement and a pile of trash outside as high as Mount Everest! It was time to inject some **lighthearted** spirit into the room.

the facelift >> Architecturally, basements are boxlike, with little or no moldings and trim, low ceilings, and if you're lucky, elongated narrow windows. According to the girls, they and their mom enjoyed evenings painting one another's nails while they watched the weepiest of movies. This new room was to be unwaveringly "girlie." It was to look like it was decorated by Barbie herself, **young, vivacious,** and **spirited.** A new birch plywood floor was nailed down because the old linoleum was irreparably damaged. Then we rolled on two coats of the most **vibrant** fuchsia floor paint. The next morning, the **happy** pink was greeted with screams of horror by the male contingent as the women looked on in Barbie heaven.

The original basement walls were covered with that typical dingy brown paneling that simply requires a **cheerful** color for an astonishing transformation. Jim, our Scottish paint hero, calmed down the pink glow by applying a contrasting golden yellow to the walls, broken up by thin pale yellow stripes spaced every 2 feet. The effect is subtle, but the vertical lines help elevate the low ceiling. **Bright** new colors were just not enough, so Jim applied a large stencil that he cut out to replicate swirls of wrought iron. It produced a **whimsical** garden detail.

By the third day, with just hours to go before Mom's return, we used **fresh** cream pink slipcovers to bring two old sofas back to life. A discarded armchair was revitalized with red and white striped fabric, and all were dressed up with a **wild** mixture of print cushions. We added several pieces of white metal garden furniture to match the walls. To create the illusion of larger windows, I called into play one of my favorite decorating tricks, which is to hang full-length curtains in front of the long narrow basement windows.

building a mood with color >> Nothing can raise the spirits like a **fresh burst** of color. The mood for this **joyful** retreat was to be **upbeat** and **fun,** and the winning combination of bright white, glowing yellow, and vibrant pink **radiates** this happy spirit.

lively facelift >>>

Emma was twenty-six years old when we were secretly contacted by her best friend. Helen explained to us how the Greek community, especially Greek fathers, are incredibly protective of their daughters. Emma had lived under her parents' roof until her endearing dad had purchased a duplex. Now the parents would live upstairs and Emma would move into the basement apartment. Finally, she would have a place of her own. Helen explained to us that Emma had been living in her new place for only a few weeks when desperation hit her hard. There were two major problems: the studio apartment was dreadful, and she had no money to orchestrate her own Facelift.

before >>

after >>

after > >

the challenge >> The basement apartment is tiny and cramped but has its own entrance, a small open kitchen, an even smaller bathroom, and a combined living and sleeping area. It's a total of 650 square feet. Although there are windows at the front and the back, the place was dark because of the wood-paneled walls. In contrast, the kitchen was more cheerful, decorated under the influence of the era with the quintessential vibrant orange tiles and countertops. But with the low ceilings and ghastly linoleum floor, it certainly did nothing to inspire a twenty-six-year-old single girl. Neither did the cast-off furnishings, which included a mishmash of pieces left from the previous occupants and donations from Mom and Dad upstairs. This was freedom at a price, and our hearts went out to Emma.

the facelift >> Our first job was to divide the living area in order to add some privacy. A wall was built down the side of the entrance stairs, and a large store-bought floor-to-ceiling bookcase was used to separate the living area from the bedroom. Plywood was attached to the back of the bookcase, and detail was added with bands of wood in a contemporary grid pattern. With the addition of a couple of reading lights, we now had not only a fabulous oversized headboard but also a small bedroom. Both sides were painted the **liveliest raspberry red.**

Extra storage cupboards were hung in the kitchen for practicality and to separate the kitchen from the living area. We decided to work with the existing orange countertops but to remove the old tile. **Vibrant orange** has made a gigantic comeback; you'll find it in home accents and accessories. We used a deep burnt orange tone on the lower cabinets and modernized the uppers with a special silver paint that creates the illusion of battered metal, both durable and stylish.

To open up the tiny kitchen further, we employed a favorite design trick. Mirrored tiles were cut into 3-inch squares, applied to the wall in the same method as ceramic tile, and grouted with the **brightest** shade of orange. **Reflection** and sheen will always produce the illusion of space, and we applied this element to the wood-paneled walls. The matte and gloss stripes, correctly named shadow stripes, visually widen and heighten the space. White cork floors were laid over the existing linoleum. Soft and warm underfoot, cork is one of my favorites for basements.

Out of desperation, we began from scratch with the furniture. The ceilings are only 8 feet high, which demanded pieces with sleek, simple lines that sit low to the floor. Once again, these details help create height and space.

building a mood with color >> The fastest way we could change the mood of Emma's studio apartment from solemn to **sunny** was with **fresh,** lively colors. Happy splashes of color—hip and retro tangerine orange in the kitchen and raspberry red on the dividing wall—give off an **invigorating** beat to the surroundings. It took four full days to inbue this unattractive, cramped space with style. Apart from the cork floor, inexpensive but modern furnishings, and a new stove, this cheerrful makeover was achieved on a limited budget using the wizardry of paint and color.

nostalgic
mood

choose a nostalgic mood . . .

All homes should capture an element of the traditional. It's the component that makes a place personal; otherwise, we might as well live in a showroom. However fabulous the sleek and trendy rooms look in the hip magazines, they have proved to be stark and even difficult to live with when personal belongings are absent. A nostalgic mood is steeped in tradition. A modern design can be comforting and warm by adding a favorite lamp that once belonged to your mother or a family photo from days gone by. When we enter a room that has been touched by history, we feel instantly at ease. These rooms hold different meanings for each of us that can include components of how and where we were brought up, a style taken from an unforgettable holiday, or travels to an exotic land. An inherited piece of furniture can warm up a corner, as will a classic wall color. Think of the way you feel when you visit a parental home, the family beach house, or lakeside cottage. These are the emotions you should try to evoke if you wish to capture this mood, whether it runs throughout every room or in one quiet corner. Textures, patterns, and colors all play key roles. Comfort is essential; be inspired by overstuffed sofas, classic fabric patterns, and wall colors that cover the spectrum, from creamy beige to royal blue. Furnishings are a visual mix of antiques, dark-hued woods, and ornate rugs. A nostalgic mood is personal, and for all of us it means a penchant for comfort.

. . . now choose a nostalgic color

Bringing a nostalgic mood to your home is all about awakening the senses. Just as a familiar smell can immediately remind you of a distant memory, so can a particular room color. The **traditional** elements are often touches from our childhood home that one day will be used in our own children's homes. This is why **classic** wall colors repeat throughout the decades, but with a new twist or combination for each era.

Blues are probably the most familiar to us and have been a favorite decorative color in most cultures and throughout the different design periods. Blue and white is a **timeless** combination. There is no fresher-looking room than one with soft blue walls and clean white woodwork and trim (see the bedroom vignette on page 80). Think of the memories evoked by a classic blue and white china pattern or a denim blue comforter and snowy white linens. Gray blues, traditionally used in century-old Swedish design, are popular for their **gentle,** familiar ambiance in today's homes. Marine blue reminds us of all things nautical, making up part of the familiar red, white, and blue trio that evokes **historic** and familial memories (see Marilyn's family room on page 99). Turquoise, with its vibrant hues, will add a splash of color

LEFT Caramel and fern green are nostalgic cousins, paired in this homey bathroom to create a fresh yet comforting mood.
OPPOSITE A single flower stalk in an unpretentious ceramic vase is reminiscent of country walks past and present.

PRECEDING PAGES, LEFT The quiet elegance of faux-stone upper walls balanced with an unusual color choice for the wainscoting transports us to another time and place.
PRECEDING PAGES, RIGHT The spectrum of creamy beiges in the faux-stone blocks brings traditional strength to a new wall.

to the plainest room. It was a favorite in the 1950s, showing up everywhere from diners to automobiles, and is now in today's homes on walls and accessories, from bowls, vases, and lamps to sinks and bathtubs.

There is an enormous spectrum of **greens,** many of which have strong connections to traditional rooms. But there are shades that go in and out of fashion. The deep hunter green once so popular in country homes now appears tired and dated. It has been replaced with warmer **sage** and fresher mossy greens.

Traditional **yellow** walls are golden, wrapping us in **elegant** warmth. Soothing yellow ocher is as vivid as it is luxurious—a good choice for sophisticated interiors. Offset with white ceilings and trim, these **rich** yellows combine effectively with dark wood antiques as well as with ornate fixtures and fittings (see the traditional living room vignette on page 83).

If you've never lived in a **red** room, I heartily suggest you try it. Although I talk about the drama of the color red on pages 110 and 111, red is also a **classic** color. Ivory-white trim combined with deep-red walls and gold accents has been a favorite for centuries. How you furnish a red room will decide how traditional or classic it will be, but a red room will always be **warm** and consoling.

The most common building materials, stone and wood, place the many shades of **gray** and **brown** solidly in the traditional spectrum. Think of the **Old World charm** of the complex beiges and grays in a stone château wall, or the deep lustrous hues of wood paneling in a den.

Balance is key to keeping white

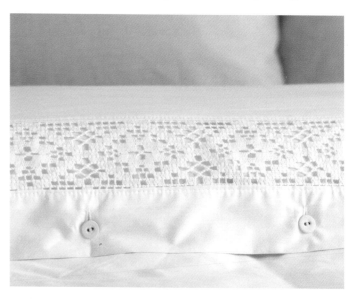

OPPOSITE, TOP This romantic bedroom combines the traditional color favorites, blue and white, with touches of heirloom handi-work. The embroidered linens, wrought-iron filigree, and Victorian-style lamp are delicate details that we embrace with a loving feeling of times past. OPPOSITE, BOTTOM Linen white emphasizes the old-fashioned lace and button details on the duvet cover.

BELOW The familiar country blue and white gingham pattern has been blown up to giant scale, and wraps the room in a youthful aura that is cheerful and inviting. Nothing else is needed on the walls. RIGHT The bedside table is a classic reminder of simple pleasures; the old-fashioned bouquet of posies, a leather-bound book, and touches of gold leaf on the painted lamp entice you to bed for quiet time.

walls harmonious with their surroundings.

tradition

comfort

vintage

The combination of **black and white** is a simple device that adds a classic touch to any room in the home. An entrance or hallway can be made architecturally prominent with a painted or tiled black and white floor in the same way a grouping of black and white frames can add **sophistication** to an otherwise plain room. The 1930s bathroom walls in city apartment buildings were often tiled in small black and white ceramics, which still look fabulous today.

Black on its own is the decorator's equivalent to fashion's little black dress. No room should be without this **grounding** element. Black's solid presence allows the colors around it to pop. It underscores the room's mood, and is part of most favorite combinations. See the effect of dark charcoal cabinets and a patterned floor in Glenn's kitchen on page 95.

OPPOSITE This mustard color is a perfect foil for the dark wood and oil paintings. Metallic accents, such as a gold pattern on the lamp shade, are traditional standards that complete the welcoming setting. The Napoleonic Bee is found on antique textiles, and is one of the oldest patterns still being replicated.

ABOVE LEFT Old World ambiance is created with the wall finish. The yellow ocher colorwash gives the walls a timeworn shading like those seen in an ancient château. **ABOVE RIGHT** The dark wood tray table and its contents could be found in any comfortable English-style sitting room. The gold printing on the books and the brass corners of the table are a match for the mottled gold wall finish.

White is a true classic and will always be imperative in some part of your home, fulfilling a nostalgic mood. Delicate white sheers and fresh white cotton lace curtains are as familiar as a summer's breeze. Crisp white bed linens have an **heirloom** quality to them. A white room can capture the **dreamy** spirit of a first snowfall. White also enhances the mystery of other colors as they reflect off a white surface. Creamy whites, taupe, and beige have been mainstays for the traditional home for the past thirty years. A new spirit can be brought to these neutrals with the mix of tiny amounts of pinks, greens, or browns. They will always be favorites because these timeless shades create **quiet** backgrounds for our furnishings and belongings.

BELOW LEFT Radiant persimmon walls, a rich dark stained floor, and stone-colored woodwork and trim have worked handsomely together for centuries.

BELOW Traditional settings are often full of intricate color and pattern. This antique crackled porcelain and bronze Chinese bowl has hints of the walls and completes this nostalgic picture.

ABOVE Thin dark red and gold bands dress up the persimmon walls and magnify the effect of the low-hung gilt-framed painting. The lace tablecloth is an heirloom that will be treasured through generations. **OPPOSITE** The crewel-work tapestry on the chair is an authentic touch, adding an air of dignity and sophistication to the striped walls.

nostalgic facelifts >>>>>

classic facelift >>

Debbie is an enthusiast of all aspects of painting and decorating. In fact, she makes her living tole painting and crafting. Her days are divided between her loving husband, Bob, their three teenage daughters, and her clients. Like so many working moms, Debbie was just too busy to find the time to tackle her own decorating dilemmas. Her biggest contention was the master bedroom. Untouched since the previous owners had occupied the room thirteen years before, it was drab and depressing. Bob and the girls wrote to me in desperation. They had watched their beloved mother drool over the beautiful results she saw on decorating shows, and it was only when her exasperation turned to tears one evening that Bob took action. An old show of mine was repeating an episode about a Jamaican plantation–inspired room. It was airy and bright with gorgeous hand-painted walls and the most romantic four-poster bed. This was his wife's dream.

before >>

after > >

lattice doors >>

This master bedroom required lots of extra space for clothes, so matching cupboards were built in on either side of the window. In keeping with the plantation-style theme, I decorated the doors with a garden lattice design. This clever trompe l'oeil effect was done with paint; the illusion of slats crossing each other is produced by the difference between the translucent glaze and opaque paint. The slats with white paint are brighter and advance, while the paler glazed slats recede.

INSTRUCTIONS

For best results, prepare your surface following the preparation tips on page 139.

step 1. Remove the doors and place them on a flat work surface.

step 2. Apply 2 base coats of pale sky blue, and let the paint dry for 4 hours.

step 3. From a large piece of vinyl, cut out a stencil to represent the slats. Cut the slats on the diagonal, moving only one way.

step 4. Use stencil spray adhesive to stick the stencil into position on the door.

step 5. Mix a white glaze, 1 part paint to 3 parts glazing liquid. Roll the translucent glaze over the stencil to produce the lower set of slats.

step 6. Remove the stencil and wipe off any leaks so your slats are neat. Let the glaze dry for at least 4 hours; you are going to stencil over it and don't want to smudge your work.

step 7. Clean the stencil, flip it over, and position it onto the door so the slats are crossing the first slats. Roll on white paint. These tops slats are brighter and will produce the illusion of depth.

step 8. Apply 2 coats of varnish to protect your finish.

the challenge >> There is usually some element —a fixture, a piece of furniture, or even the floor covering—that can be salvaged, but in Debbie and Bob's bed and bath, there were no redeeming features. This was a complete gutting job—nothing would be spared. Out came the carpet, their old bed, the blinds, and the whole bathroom. However short of space you are, a closet is never a practical idea in a bathroom because of the daily moisture buildup. The old shower, toilet, and sink were scrapped along with the closet. We had an empty shell.

the facelift >> The old bathroom and bedroom floors were covered during the first night with solid wood planks that literally click into place. In the bathroom, a platform was built to house a new tub, and a vanity was built from scratch for the new sink. A modern walled-in shower would replace the plastic one, and all these surfaces would be covered with mustard-yellow mosaic tile. An oversized framed mirror was hung above the sink, but the focal point of the small bathroom was Jim's mural. He painted enormous tropical leaves around the walls.

While the resurrection of the new bathroom took place, the bedroom was also receiving a **revival** with a **Colonial** touch. The new dark wood

after >>

before >>

floors grounded the space, especially with the **traditional paper** that I chose for the walls. We first nailed sheets of Masonite around the lower half of the room, and then dressed it up with molding around the bottom and the top. Every 2½ feet we added a length of molding, which imitates the look of **classic** paneling, especially when glossed up with two coats of white paint. Wall panels are reminiscent of old English style or the breezy ambiance of a Cape Cod beach home. The wallpaper is a **historical English damask pattern** that is once again being introduced to an ever-growing market. The highlight of the room is the four-poster bed; it's always a favorite. Once made from solid mahogany, the new ones found in stores today are constructed of less expensive woods and then stained, yet still cost thousands of dollars. For approximately $600, we made our own, and smothered it in pure white linens with accents of yellow. The bed is spectacular. The rest of the room was left relatively simple—white flowing curtains and a few pieces of **vintage** dark furniture. Debbie did need closet space, since we had demolished her only source. Two large built-in armoires were dressed up to match the bathroom vanity, mimicking the décor of a Caribbean plantation house.

building a mood with color >>
Creamy yellow will always have a **time-honored** traditional flare. Partnered with white paneling, the style is **old** yet new.

<< four-poster bed

Debbie's dream of a plantation bedroom would not have been complete without the magnificent four-poster bed. The posts were made from parts found at the lumber store; a porch column, a railing, and a pineapple finial make up each post. Use wood dowels and carpenter's glue to make strong joins between the post sections. I wanted the posts to look as though they had been carved from real mahogany, so I painted a rust-red base coat directly onto the bare pine, then brushed on a dark walnut stain, and wiped it back with a soft rag so that the red base shone through. I repeated the stain step until I had a deep mahogany color, and finished with coats of semigloss varnish that gleam in both day and night light.

handsome facelift >>

There are always e-mails that leap out from the crowd, and Pat's was one of them. As the head of an extraordinary household, she captured our attention. Pat was hoping to surprise her ex-husband with a kitchen Facelift. We were intrigued. We met with Pat and she explained her dilemma. She and Glenn, once married, share a seventeen-year-old daughter, Kim. Pat is now married to Mike and they have two young children, Sean and Kelly. Ex-husband Glenn lives around the corner from Pat and her new family, and visits every day for breakfast on his way to work and then again for dinner on his way home. Although Glenn was

before >>

always welcome in her home, Pat blamed his inability to cook for himself on the state of his kitchen—it was depressing. The *Facelift* team was on a mission to remodel Glenn's sad old kitchen into an art piece that would inspire him to cook.

after > >

<< tuscan **faux brick**

In this stunning kitchen renovation, the inset brick archway was first framed with drywall and plywood. Wiring was put in place and holes were cut for three pot lights under the arch. The "bricks" were made with Spacco, a plaster with a bit of sand in it.

step 1. Measure and tape off the brick border in the shape of an arch. Apply a coat of plaster with a trowel or metal spatula to cover the border area.

step 2. While the plaster is still wet, tape off the brick shapes. Rip the edges of the tape so that the grouting will look uneven and realistic.

step 3. Apply a second coat of plaster over the tape. Roll over the plaster with a stucco roller to create texture.

step 4. Remove the tape while the plaster is still wet, revealing the brick shapes.

step 5. Let the plaster dry. Apply a base coat of pale gray paint the color of grout to the whole surface, making sure to get into the grout lines made by the tape in Step 3.

step 6. Dry-brush shades of terra-cotta and cream paint onto the bricks to build up authentic coloring.

the challenge >> At no more than 14 square feet, Glenn's kitchen was small, bland, and unused. The year-old stove was still pristine and the new fridge stocked only beer and wine. The cabinets were unchanged since the '40s and the floor probably last had any attention at about the same time. The *Facelift* team had a blank canvas, but with a limited budget we needed to spend our money wisely.

the facelift >> The first major task in the kitchen was the removal of the upper cabinets. Glenn would lose storage space, but since his collection of kitchenware was minimal, we guessed this was irrelevant. With the Facelift we had in mind, what he lost in storage he would gain in a feeling of space and **grandeur.** The old countertops were in appalling shape, so they would be replaced with sleek walnut. This **luscious wood** makes a sumptuous focal point and is where we spent most of the budget.

Before the cabinets and counter were tackled, the arch was built. Jim, our specialty painter and whiz with plaster, was to turn a plywood arch built by Paul and Jason into Tuscan brick. The arch juts out from the wall by about 14 inches, adding an illusion of depth to the room. The faux bricks are formed from decorative plaster. It looks just like the real thing, but at a fraction of the cost.

The carpenters built a shelving unit within the archway that would house a microwave, since Glenn had yet to master the stove. The old lower cabinets remained, but look brand new; we restyled the doors with wood borders and painted them a sexy charcoal gray. The idea for the floor was to replicate old English tile floors, but we used comfortable and less costly vinyl instead. We asked a flooring company that specializes in good-quality vinyl to cut brown, black, and tan geometric

shapes to imitate the old tile. The effect is stunning. To ensure that Glenn would be able to take advantage of his new kitchen, we completed the Facelift by stocking up on cookware, essential utensils, and back-to-basics cookbooks.

building a mood with color >>
All the colors in the kitchen carry a **touch of history.** The bricks are a blend of **earthy shades** reminiscent of the Tuscan countryside, and the black, brown, and tan patterned floor is **old English.** Charcoal gray is a **classic** that grounds the lower cabinets.

family facelift >>

We receive thousands of letters and e-mails from viewers wishing for a home Facelift. The majority of pleas come from women desperate to surprise their husbands. Truthfully, we all know who is really craving that new kitchen or fancy boudoir. Marilyn's e-mail was typical of this tack. She said they had lived with their dated family room for far too long and her husband just hated to go in there. Right. We told her we would take a look, but no promises— our usual response. We poked around the room with tape measures and a video camera, making some incidental notes. And then, unkindly, we told Marilyn her home was not presently suitable for a Facelift, but we'd keep her on our list. Maybe she would have a better chance in a few years. Crestfallen, she let us out.

before >>

after > >

the challenge >> The family room was typical of those built in the mid-'80s with its soaring cathedral ceiling, brick fireplace, huge windows, and far too much dingy wood. The problem with these lofty spaces is that they are all walls and windows, and because of this we tend to be afraid to use color. This misconception ensures that we stay hiding behind builder's beige instead of using fabulous color to its best advantage. The focal point of this room is the brick wall. Towering from floor to ceiling, it dominates the space. The entire family room, including the outdated furnishings, was awkward. I understood why Marilyn hated it.

the facelift >> Marilyn and Jack's now-grown children, Eviva, Brian, and Rebecca, had been brought up in this room surrounded by the furnishings, so they felt nostalgic and reluctant to change anything. But they had all moved out and this Facelift was for Marilyn, so I made most of the decorating decisions. I was aiming toward a **traditional welcoming** family room that displayed a lifetime of **memories** in a warm yet upbeat fashion. We began at the top and painted the dark beamed wood ceiling flat white, immediately brightening the room. The old pot lights were replaced by oversized wrought-iron chandeliers spray-painted white and hung on chains.

The kids were against touching the brick wall, but the flat expanse was monotonous. I broke up the space by adding bleached wood paneling and a mantel that was then toned down with a light colorwash. Next came the wall color. This would dominate the space, so why be shy? I chose a **heritage** red, **formal but vibrant.** As soon as the paint was on, the entire ambiance changed.

floors >>

Since time is always short on *Facelift* shows, we have come to rely on "floating floors." This is a relatively new system of laying floors that we can all attempt ourselves; no nails or glue are required, just measuring and cutting each length. The prefinished wood, cork, bamboo, vinyl, or laminate planks have tongue and groove edges that click together. These floors are fast and easy to install and can be laid over cement, plywood, or old wooden floors.

Now we needed a special floor that would ground the high ceiling. For speed, we chose a floating wood floor that just clicks into place, but instead of the standard uniform color, we picked two shades, a dark brown and a soft honey, and laid them in a striped pattern. The room was completed with **timeless navy** slipcovers for the original sofas now rearranged for a more **intimate** layout. We made an oversized mirror framed with stock molding, which brought the room to scale by breaking up what was left of the high brick wall. The metal Venetian blinds were replaced with beige linen dressed up with a wide band of navy—**classic colors with a fresh young twist.** The room captivates the spirit of this family.

building a mood with color >>

Plenty of sun-bleached wood and a nautical color scheme for paint and fabrics work well to produce a **homey, nostalgic** mood in the two-story living room.

memorable facelift >>

Jodi and Luigi had bought their first house as newlyweds a year before. They dreamed of making their house—one of hundreds of identical units—a home, one that would stand out in the crowd. The plain white walls began to get Jodi down, but Luigi was so busy at work that he had no time to get involved. Jodi wrote to us looking for a solution. We loved this story because it was so common, but there was a catch. We were all surprised the next day to receive another e-mail, this time from Luigi. He heartbreakingly explained how his wife felt that he wasn't interested in their home, but he just did not know how to help her. Could we help him?

before > >

after > >

the challenge >> In keeping with today's architecture, the house had an open plan, one room leading into the next. This was their dilemma: Where to start? Could they use more than one color? The list of problems was endless, and so they acted like so many of us and did nothing. The challenge was to pick a color scheme that would work throughout the ground floor of the house.

the facelift >> We chose three different tones of gray, and by contrasting the **warmth** of the pine floors and the ocher fireplace with the cool grays of the walls, the home took on a **timeless quality.** The lightest gray was applied in a satin finish to the entrance hall, a slightly darker tone to the dining area in the same sheen; we also added this color to the small section of wall showing in the kitchen. The living room walls were painted in a dark gray, and to add depth and a **seductive** quality to the space, three coats of high-gloss varnish were applied. This **reflective** surface allows the living area to stand out from the dining room and hallway, but at the same time blends with the rest of the ground floor.

Their fireplace was an unappealing surround of tile, not an interesting focal point. We boxed in the tiles with plywood and at the same time built a step to ground the firebox. Then we attached two decorative wooden sconces to the new surround **reminiscent** of **traditional** fireplaces. The mantel was given a faux-wood effect to match the sconces, and the rest of the mantel was covered with an exterior plaster, then rubbed with ocher

<< faux-**wood plank**

Each type of wood has its own color and character. When you are planning to reproduce the look of wood planks, it's helpful to study the real thing, or a photograph or lifelike illustration, to learn the variations in grain, knotholes, and shades. Wood's markings and coloration also change over time as it weathers and wears.

There are many ways to reproduce the look of wood. Wood-graining tools, called rockers, leave realistic markings when they are pulled through wet glaze. To give the illusion of age and wear, you can beat up the surface; use a sharp nail or screw to drag scratch marks and a hammer and nail to make holes.

For Luigi's fireplace, I mixed brown paint and high-gloss varnish to turn a piece of drywall into a glossy block of wood. The transparent property of the varnish allows the base coat to shine through and actually illuminates the wood's color. You can use the same method on a plywood, metal, or laminate surface. Use the proper primer to prepare the surface for paint (see A Professional Finish, page 140).

INSTRUCTIONS

For best results, prepare your surface following the preparation tips on page 139.

step 1. Apply 2 base coats of a mustard orange color, and let them dry for 4 hours.

step 2. Mix equal parts of dark brown paint and high-gloss varnish. Brush on the colored varnish, covering 100 percent of the surface.

step 3. Push the brush through the wet varnish to make grain lines. Move in one direction, horizontally. The lines will not all be straight. Do not overwork this effect. Faux wood is most realistic when it is applied subtly.

glaze. An easy trick to add **architectural detail** to newer homes is with moldings. Instead of applying them just to the walls, we nailed a 4-inch separate strip of molding into the ceiling. This technique was applied throughout the ground floor, linking all the rooms together.

Our next big job was the entrance hall. We dressed up the windows to make an unusual but welcoming statement. A mirror was suspended from the ceiling in front of the window. The small area was made special by stenciling a three-dimensional, circular border onto the ceiling and filling in the center with a painted sky. I added some sparkle to their dining room set by making a flamboyant movable top for their table. The tabletop was then painted in a zebra pattern, which is **whimsical** but also **classic.**

building a mood with color >>
Using shades of gray and varying the sheen from flat to gloss adds a **modern twist on a traditional look.** The addition of **moldings** and painted accents gives a **sense of history** to a new home.

<< paint a **sky**

The calm and whimsical nature of a painted sky makes it a popular choice for ceilings. There are a few tips that will help you to create the illusion of clouds floating by overhead. The background blue can be applied as a solid base coat or broken up with a colorwash. Clouds appear to be brighter where the sun highlights them, so use denser white along the tops. The shading is what brings the picture to life. A white glaze and a little umber or pink glaze will help to produce gradation in color and movement.

Not many homes today can take a whole ceiling of painted sky. Instead, why not paint a small vignette on the ceiling such as I did in Luigi's hallway? The illusion of a framed skylight is simply produced with paint and stencils. After filling in the sky, two stencils were used for the frame. One is the molding pattern and the second stencil is placed to make realistic shading for a three-dimensional effect. This stencil is called an overlay.

INSTRUCTIONS

For best results, prepare your surface following the preparation tips on page 139.

step 1. Paint the background with 2 base coats of sky blue (here I used a light baby blue), and let the paint dry for 4 hours.

step 2. If you are making a skylight, use low-tack painter's tape to mask off the boundaries where the frame will go.

step 3. Mix a very transparent white glaze, 3 parts glazing liquid to 1 part white paint. Use this runny white paint for drawing in the shape and direction of the clouds. They should have some form and movement and look as if they are all blowing in one direction.

step 4. Use thick white latex paint to plump up some of the clouds.

step 5. For a realistic highlight, brush on small areas of ocher color to suggest that the sun has caught the clouds.

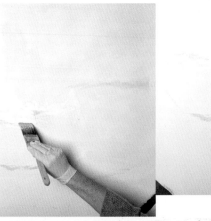

develop a

dramatic
mood

choose a dramatic mood . . . There are some rooms that cry out to be noticed; they take center stage; they crave compliments. Dramatic spaces bring out the extrovert in some of us, the passion in others. A strong statement through the play of color, lighting, and furnishings tells the world—or a least your friends and family—that this is a place in which to be confident and motivated. When we talk about dramatic moods, dining rooms come to mind immediately. The décor can enhance the ambiance whether with a theatrical theme or a luxurious display of colors and textures. Guests will be aroused to vibrant conversation and laughter. This bold

mood makes us sit up a little straighter and lose our shyness. It even quickens our heartbeat as the space alerts our senses. This excitable state may not be your first thought in the bedroom, but alluring colors and textures can do much to stimulate an erotic atmosphere: love and passion are always dramatic. If this intense mood is scary but does interest you, then try it on a smaller space such as the bathroom. Start the day with vigor and conviction in a bathroom that makes you feel mighty and strong, with an intensity that says today you can tackle anything. In the living room, small bursts of energy can be achieved with rich accents such as jewel-toned cushions or metallic touches. A mood that is both playful and dramatic should be bold but not overpowering.

. . . now choose a dramatic color

Colors that have a delightful energy are usually dense, deeply saturated tones. They must be used carefully to ensure that they **invigorate**, not overpower. A **dramatic** palette can be inspirational in a picture, but for many, these strong colors are intimidating choices for our own homes. However, these dominant colors, used with a successful combination of fabrics and furnishings, offer a delightful surprise.

Hot orange, **vivid** reds, burgundies, and pinks are the most dazzlingly sensuous group of colors. There is a primal energy and heat associated with these hues that taps into our own passionate spirit.

Reds run the gamut from demure to sexy, exotic to dangerously **wild**. I believe we should all enjoy the intensity of a red room at some stage in our lives. The eye is immediately drawn to red, so imagine the impact and intrigue

LEFT A monotone palette with different textures (found in the fabric weaves, paint, and furnishings) presents many seductive levels of interest. **FAR LEFT** Sensuous fabrics in glorious tones of red set up an opulent mood in this bedroom. The mix of cotton, chenille, linen, and silk contrasts rustic and fine weaves in an enticing and luxurious setting.

PRECEDING PAGES, LEFT Stenciling large, turquoise palm leaves across a raspberry wall takes a courageous soul. Velvet and silk curtains are always luxurious. With this combination of potent color and tactile materials, you are ready for any adventure. **PRECEDING PAGES, RIGHT** Both these saturated colors are bold, one cool and the other warm. Candlelight is a must.

Fiery or **spicy** orange will always cast a captivating glow.

ABOVE Vibrant burnt orange walls wake up the spirit, and the black wainscoting punctuates the color. The thoughtful balance of opposites is pure theater. **RIGHT** The brushed-metal box sitting on white tile would be cool and contemporary, but the orange and red woven mat changes the mood dramatically.

OPPOSITE, TOP The black border highlights the difference between a common brown basket weave and a startling selection of colored towels. **OPPOSITE, BOTTOM** The graduation in color on the upper walls from light to dark is reminiscent of a fiery sunset. The solid black wainscoting and brown woven baskets are masculine and deceptively simple counterparts.

exciting

of catching a glimpse of a red room as you enter a home. A whole room painted red is as welcoming as a single red wall in an otherwise neutral space. Be cautious, though, because an abundance of red can be exhausting and aggressive in a well-used room. To cool down the vibrancy of the red tones, balance the room with trim and accessories in white and cream. Dark wood furniture and a sumptuous fabric such as velvet will complement the luxurious ambiance. A dark glaze over the top of a red base coat (see Mrs. Biggs's bedroom on page 129) will create an intimacy and warmth that is ideal for a master bedroom.

Orange is both **dramatic** and cheerful and will create a lighter mood than red. Fiery or spicy orange will always cast a captivating glow, **empowering** family and guests with confidence. It is tough to be in a bad mood in an orange space. Balance these **vibrant** colors with the starkness of white or contrasting blues to tame their vigor. Or ground the **energy** of an orange room with the weight of a dark charcoal floor (see Karen and Pierre's kitchen on page 121).

Strong yellows are **intense** and have become a favorite in stark modern lofts to uplift and add a theatrical tone to the space. Bright acid yellow is both mentally stimulating and aggressive and should be toned down with the strength of black or white. Bright yellows literally glow with life. They will enliven a dark kitchen with gusto.

Deep blues radiate an extraordinary power. We associate sparkling sapphire blue with wealth and

Bright acid yellow is both mentally stimulating and aggressive

beauty, royal blue connotes regal attention, and navy blue signifies order.
These important shades of blue are
cool and somber on their own, but
paired with white, they lighten up and
glow (see the dramatic living room on
page 117). Cobalt blue is clean and
fresh, stunning as an exterior paint
color especially for a summer cottage.
In the cabana on page 125 we contrasted this blue with the tang of lime
green to strike a mood reminiscent of
the vibrant Caribbean.

The combination of black and
white is theatrical and powerful but
must be used with care. Black will
sharpen other color schemes, but too
much black can be somber. A wall

ABOVE The electric yellow wall delivers shock value, especially behind the minimalist black and white décor. Carefully chosen elements leave nothing to
chance; a crisp white linen tablecloth, exotic grasses in a tall black vase, and
simple bowls heaped with fresh greens await a confident urban personality. The
painted white floor reflects the lively burst of yellow and ensures the tempo is
upbeat.

OPPOSITE White now outweighs black, and the room feels lighter and more fanciful. The bright lemon background has been somewhat softened by a randomly
stenciled damask pattern. The unorthodox white and black chair is eye-catching.
RIGHT The solid black tabletop grounds the floating features of the wall, glass,
and candles.

and should be toned down with the strength of black or white.

adventurous

theatrical

papered in an oversized black and white print will add drama, as will a few silhouettes of interestingly shaped black objects in an all-white room.

White, although not truly a color, is **powerful** as it reflects the ever-changing light and its surroundings. The intensity of pure white is emotional and **theatrical**, but to avoid the pure minimalist look, mix it with a variety of textures, woods, and materials.

ABOVE LEFT The artful display of tropical fruit against the dramatic blue and white walls is reminiscent of island pleasures. **ABOVE RIGHT** There's no hidden agenda here. Judging from the stack of travel books and the collection of rocks, travel is a passion. This is a personal space for an adventurer to dream.

LEFT Navy blue on its own is cool and intense, like a midnight sky. A balanced dose of white from the stark furnishings lightens the room, but the mood remains thoughtful and discriminating.

OPPOSITE This bold take on traditional navy and white stripes is fearless and flamboyant. Geometry is at play as our eyes are drawn to the many clean lines—while the cushion fabric offers a stunning change.

dramatic facelifts >>>>>

flamboyant facelift >>

Karen and Pierre had been living in their first house for about a year. It was known by family and friends as "the white house," and not because of its importance. The exterior of this small Cape Cod–style house was white, as was every room inside. The couple disliked white but they couldn't agree on anything, let alone a color scheme. Pierre, a snowboarding fanatic, told us that Karen was a **high-energy** woman who adored **exciting** colors. However, she needed a gentle prod to give her the courage to tackle each room. That nudge came from the *Facelift* team. We began the process of surprising her by adding color to her kitchen and the adjoining den.

before >>

after > >

the challenge >> A kitchen is the most costly room to renovate, so it was here and in the adjoining den that we could make the most dramatic change. Standard white laminate cabinets and wood trim dominated the room, along with all-white appliances. The floors were dated parquet throughout. They had made one mutual and successful decorating decision: they'd purchased a mossy-green sectional for the den. That's all that would stay.

the facelift >> The first job was to remove some of the upper cabinets in order to allow the room to breathe. The cabinets that were left were extended to the ceiling by keeping the skeleton but replacing the doors with taller ones that would give an illusion of height to the room.

While the carpentry was in full swing, I showed Pierre the color scheme. If we had not already destroyed the old kitchen, I believe he would have called the whole thing off. We had chosen **vibrant tones** of orange; Pierre was in shock. After a lengthy persuasive discussion about trust and faith, the work continued. The orange paint was applied in blocks on the ceiling and walls, linking the two open spaces and solving the problem of the uneven ceiling. The upper cabinets were also orange, but instead of paint, a **wild** laminate in **swirls and flames** of **fiery orange** was glued in place and then secured further with aluminum trim. Deep charcoal melamine paint was rolled over the old laminate countertops as well as the lower cabinets.

The biggest expense was the dark gray slate cut into subway tiles for the backsplash. The carpenters, Paul and Jason, built two very different tables to suit Karen and Pierre's lifestyle. A large table decorated with slate tiles gives eat-in **glamour** to the kitchen, and for the den, there was a stylish free-form coffee table on wheels. Both the kitchen and den were finished with a patterned vinyl floor in the darkest gray.

I added two **unique ideas** to this space. The first was an amazing way of boxing in a plain white refrigerator. Jason housed it in a medium-density fiber-board surround; then lengths of pine were attached in even stripes around the casing. Everything was painted white; the effect is architecturally stylish. The second solution was for the lighting. We fixed desk lamps to the ceiling that could be turned on by the main wall switch.

building a mood with color >> **Flamboyant** and cheerful, orange is not for the faint of heart. It's a **powerful** choice that will keep conversation and **energy levels high.** We conjured up a **dramatic** contemporary setting in the kitchen and adjoining den with the juxtaposition of **hot orange** and cool white and charcoal applied in sections or blocks.

before > >

after > >

artistic facelift >>

Partners for more than sixteen years, Toby and DJ opted for a simpler lifestyle after the disaster of the World Trade Center attacks. DJ found an old farm far away from city life but close enough to New York so Toby, a successful Broadway producer, could continue to run his company and periodically commute to the city. DJ would run the farm. Toby's organizational skills, which his career has depended on, played a major role in orchestrating a cast of approximately forty people during a hot and sticky June week in the country. When we first secretly visited, we discovered it was not the farmhouse that Toby had in mind for *Facelift*. Instead, we were greeted at the door of a small milking shed.

before >>

after > >

the challenge >> Unused for years, the milking shed sadly stood surrounded by larger, more impressive barns. Although it had a slight tilt, the shed was structurally sound with prime views of woods and fields. Toby's dream was to demolish the interior and create a beach-style cabana. My dream was to run from the mouse-infested structure immediately. However, the promise of a week down on the farm was far too enticing for the *Facelift* team, so with chain saws, diggers, back hoes, and even a tractor we began our most adventurous makeover.

the facelift >> The first couple of days were spent in a hive of activity as the interior was torn out of the old milking shed. The ceiling was removed, opening it up to the tin roof, which immediately made the area more spacious. Paul and Derek laid out all the wide old planks **salvaged** from the ceiling, which would eventually be cleaned up and reused for

rugged doors, a giant coffee table, and deep, lounging sofas. Once the cow pens, hay, and remnants of broken-down farm equipment were removed, we were left with a dismal mess of a floor. The concrete was badly cracked. It's not that I was hoping for a perfect floor—this was a shed, after all—but I was expecting one that was at least capable of supporting furniture without being wobbly. We racked our brains for a solution until some genius came up with the idea of using driveway concrete. Even better, we then found a company that stencils patterns onto driveways using colored concrete and enormous stencils.

Toby wanted a retreat that was relaxing and at the same time a little **out-rageous,** a place that **made you smile** on entering. I gave him a **bold** color palette that would make anyone grin from to ear to ear. First the wood plank walls were painted a **lively lemon-green** on the inside and **cobalt blue** on the outside. Then the original concrete floor was stenciled with colored concrete in a **mango-tinted giraffe pattern.**

While the interior work battled ahead, we brought in a garden team headed by Kim, my landscape buddy. They built a deck stained in the same **luscious** blue as the outside of the cabana. This was surrounded by a small garden with its own fountain carved out of a large boulder and a fire pit for chilly evenings.

The cabana was filled with **oversized** lounging sofas made from the original shed planks and covered with futons and masses of cushions. A series of long mirrors was dressed up with a frosted-leaf effect that reflects the natural beauty and light of the outdoors.

building a mood with color >> Situated in the wide open space of a rural landscape, the shed-turned-cabana had plenty of space to breathe, so

we took a rather unorthodox approach to produce a **fanciful** and **dramatic** mood. We matched up two of nature's most common duos, blue and green. We chose a lively **acid green** for the interior walls, a **stimulating** color that can be shocking, but the colored accents keep it balanced and light. The big surprise is the **cobalt blue** exterior, a **strong** and **glorious** color that works magically with the surroundings.

theatrical facelift >>

Mrs. Biggs is an English teacher adored and respected by a generation of pupils for her outstanding teaching methods. Mrs. Biggs is also the homeroom teacher to twenty-two eleventh-grade boys who approached me about giving Mrs. Biggs a Facelift. According to the kids, she had two passions apart from Mr. Biggs—teaching and fashion. The boys always looked forward to her English class, not just for Mrs. Biggs's enthusiasm for literature but also for her eclectic dress sense. According to the students, she had never worn the same outfit twice. This I found rather unbelievable until the boys showed me a video project that had been filmed the previous year entitled *The Horrors of Mrs. Biggs's Closet.* After contacting Mr. Biggs and getting his approval for the adventure, we received the go-ahead to redecorate and reorganize their bedroom, with the added task of building his wife a new and enlarged closet.

before > >

after > >

<< frottage

The name stems from the French verb, *frotter*, which means "to rub." But don't let the fancy label discourage you; this is not a difficult effect to produce, although I do recommend working with a partner.

To achieve the look, a solid coat of colored glaze is rolled on over a slightly lighter colored base coat. Sheets of craft paper are pressed onto the wet glazed surface and gently rubbed, then removed. Some of the glaze is pulled away, leaving behind on the wall gradations in color and creases. This is a sophisticated effect that suits dark, rich colors such as mustard, brown, or red.

INSTRUCTIONS

For best results, prepare your surface following the preparation tips on page 139.

step 1. Apply 2 base coats of medium red to the surface and let dry for 4 hours. Dark colors may need 3 or 4 coats for full coverage.

step 2. Mix the glaze, 1 part dark red latex paint to 3 parts water-based glazing liquid. Scrunch up several pieces of craft paper and then flatten them out again.

step 3. Roll the colored glaze onto the wall from the top to the bottom in a strip as wide as the craft paper sheets. The glaze should cover 100 percent of the work section.

step 4. Press the paper onto the wet glaze, rubbing the paper down gently with flat fingers.

step 5. Immediately remove the paper.

step 6. Roll more colored glaze onto the next section of the wall, overlapping the edge of the previously worked glaze so that you don't get lap lines (see A Professional Finish, page 140).

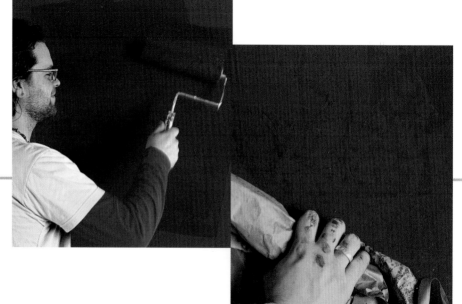

the challenge >> The boys were right! Mrs. Biggs's closet was stressed to the limit. Clothes were jammed along racks and spilled from shelving. More than seventy pairs of shoes were stacked in piles; accessories were hung from every hook. The bedroom was drab, with plain white walls, a dated wallpaper border, and matching curtain frills.

the facelift >> The first job was to knock out the existing closet door and open up the wall, enabling us to put in double doors. Although this meant losing about 3 feet of wall space inside, it also makes the closet more open and storage space more accessible.

While the newly plastered opening was drying, the wallpaper border was removed, and the four-poster bed was redesigned by cutting off the original cane headboard and replacing it with a handsome new one. Plywood was cut into a stepped shape and then upholstered in the deepest plum imitation suede. It was finished with two lines of upholstery studs. The **dramatic new headboard** was designed to complement the anticipated ambiance of the bedroom—with shape, color, and texture all contributing. The intention was to capitalize on Mrs. Biggs's **stylish** lifestyle and envelop her in a bedroom that was both **luxurious** and **flamboyant.**

The color scheme of deep reds and plums contrasted with a pure white ceiling and crisp, clean linens. The base coat of **rich, cranberry red** was applied first, then mixed with a **plum-colored glaze.** A giggling group of teenage boys was given the opportunity to practice their first paint effect, called frottage, on their teacher's walls. The effect is an illusion of walls covered in **lush red velvet.** Even the lads loved it. These **sophisticated** walls were trimmed with a bronze foil molding.

bronze foil on molding >>

Metallic foil is a less expensive alternative to leaf, and because it is less fragile, it's easier to apply. Gilding with foil is a beautiful way to highlight the intricate carvings and indentations in architectural brackets and moldings.

INSTRUCTIONS

For best results, prepare your surface following the preparation tips on page 139. Match up the color of the metallic base coat to the bronze foil as closely as possible.

step 1. Apply a base coat of dark bronze metallic paint to 100 percent of the surface, and let it dry for 4 hours. Brush on the size (gilding glue), making sure to get into all the nooks and indentations. Let it dry to the tacky stage.

step 2. Lay down the foil over the molding, using a rag to press the leaf into the indentations. As you pull off the foil, the metal layer is left behind on the surface.

step 3. Apply 2 coats of varnish for protection.

Thick velvet curtains trimmed with a band of **luscious brocade** were hung on bronze rods.

While one group of classmates helped us in the bedroom, the rest learned the skills needed for basic carpentry. To the boys' immense pleasure, they helped Paul and Derek build shelves and railings and install ready-made drawers into a dressing room **fit for a queen.** The entire wood surface was painted the deepest eggplant and accessorized with brass fittings. With a mixture of task lighting (the bedside lamps) and ambient light (a chandelier), the red bedroom and en suite dressing room create a mood of thespian standards.

building a mood with color >>
Deep tones of red and luscious plum are both **passionate** colors. The crushed-velvet paint texture on the walls is made more **glamorous** topped by carved, golden moldings.

prime time

Tips and Techniques for Completing Your Own Facelifts

take action

Just like the *Facelift* shows, your home makeovers will be only as successful as the planning that goes into every step. It all begins with a dream, and then, to reach the goal, you need an action plan. I have shown you many exciting before-and-after room scenarios throughout this book. The design and decorating dilemmas in each home are common ones—poor use or lack of space, dark surroundings, dated materials—and these challenges always need to be resolved within a budget.

The pressure of an unrealistically tight time frame is an integral feature of the show, since the makeovers are a surprise. We, however, have lots of help; I do *not* recommend that you try this at home by yourself. But the transformations are very real and accessible to everyone who wants a change for the better. Map out a strategy, learn as much as you can about the different aspects of your ensuing makeover, draw up a schedule that makes sense for your life, and forge ahead. The anticipation and the excitement of achieving your goal are powerful stimulants.

your dream

Having the dream is the first, most important stage. Be inspired by the world around you: favorite haunts both nearby and faraway, settings and styles seen in movies, books, and magazines. What are the colors and moods that continually tug at your heart? Is there a room in which you have felt utterly comfortable, happy, and welcome?

Search your imagination for those elements that you require. It may be the simplicity of unadorned furnishings in warm neutral hues circling a chic fireplace; it could be the jumble of books and photographs surrounding a magnificent bed layered in exotic linens. Think big. There are numerous ways to accommodate your wishes for the space you live in, no matter what the size, the condition, or the location.

make a plan

Once you have an overall mood or theme in mind, look critically at what your present living space has to offer and what can be changed. If you want a more open layout, can you remove a wall? If you live in tight quarters, built-ins and dual-purpose partitions are great space-saving solutions. Custom-built furnishings, such as tables and benches, can be designed and finished to enhance the style you love. Plain walls can be given character with moldings and trim, and even sheets of ply-wood as well as paint and plaster finishes.

Write down the to-do list, along with the materials to gather together, and names and phone numbers of any addi-tional helping hands. It's a good idea to stipulate the approximate time each step will take, or even the particular days you have planned to put aside for each job. This is your game plan; each step finished brings you closer to your dream room.

create a mood with color

Rolling on a few coats of paint is all you need to transform the look, feel, and style of any room. Even on the tightest budget, the entire mood of the room can be altered with a coat of fresh paint on the walls. You can purchase paint in hundreds of colors, and its cost, availability, and versatility make it an indispensable tool for any decorator.

Paint is an opaque medium that forms a skin on top of the surface and covers up what is underneath. Latex and acrylic paints are both water based; they are more environmentally friendly than oil-based paints, they have little odor, and they dry almost immediately, which makes them today's popular choice for home decorating. Unless otherwise noted, I have used water-based paint products throughout this book.

By manipulating paint when it is on the surface, you create a paint effect. Paint effects add texture, pattern, and design to any surface. With a little paint you can imitate more expensive materials such as wood, granite, and stone. However, in order to be able to move around water-based paint before it dries, it is necessary to mix it with glazing liquid to form a colored glaze.

>> Clean surfaces of loose dirt, grease, and grime.

glaze

Water-based glazing liquid has a milky color, but it dries clear. It has two important properties that boost the versatility of paint. When it is mixed with paint, it makes the opaque paint translucent. This means that when you apply a colored glaze (paint-glaze mix) over a plain-paint base coat, you will see the base color shine through, creating layers of color. The glaze gives the flat color dimension.

The second property relates to the need for the longer time required for producing a pattern with water-based paints. Glazing liquid has extenders in it that retard the drying time, so that you can produce a paint effect.

The more glaze added to paint, the more translucent the colored glaze will be

preparation **tips** >>

The first step in achieving success with a paint or plaster effect is proper surface preparation. Take the extra time early in the process and your work will not only last a long time, it will also make you proud.

>> Clean surfaces of loose dirt, grease, and grime. Use soap and water and dry the surfaces thoroughly before proceeding with a primer or paint.

>> If you are removing wallpaper, wash off any glue residue.

>> For stubborn soil, or to remove the shine from slippery surfaces such as laminates, melamine, Formica, or tile, use a strong cleanser such as TSP.

>> Repair nail holes and small cracks with spackle, let dry, and sand smooth.

>> If you are not sure whether the walls were previously painted with oil or water-based paint, apply an oil-based primer. You can apply latex paint over an oil-based primer, but not over oil-based paint.

>> Use a high-hide primer to cover a dark color as well as water stains and indelible marks.

>> Use a good-quality, high-adhesive primer for slippery surfaces such as paint with a glossy sheen and laminates.

>> New drywall, freshly plastered walls, and wall repairs must be primed.

>> It is not necessary to strip wood furniture down to raw wood before repainting. Sand the piece to rough up the surface, clean away the sanding dust, and repair any small holes or cracks with wood filler. Then apply a high-adhesion primer.

and the longer it will take to dry. Conversely, if you want a more opaque mix, add more paint. Recipes for the paint-glaze mix are included as required for each of the paint effect's instructions.

When applying paint effects such as colorwashing and frottage, it is necessary to work in manageable patches of 3 or 4 square feet at a time so that you will be able to produce the desired overall effect without leaving lap lines. If the colored glaze dries between sections before you have had a chance to complete the effect, roll a little clear glazing liquid over the join to open it up.

a professional finish

Once you have properly prepared your surfaces, and the base coat has been applied, you are ready to apply the paint effect.

Work on one wall at a time and tape off the adjoining walls so that you won't get paint buildup in the corners. Start at the top of the wall and work down in 3- or 4-square foot sections. When you reach the bottom, return to the top and work down again. Apply the colored glaze to the first section, work the effect, and then apply the colored glaze to the next section, overlapping the edge slightly to ensure that it is wet. Work the effect starting at the edge and complete that section. Continue in this manner until the wall is finished.

If an edge becomes dry before it is worked, roll on some clear glaze to open it up. It is important to move quickly, and it helps if you can work with a partner— one person applying the glaze, the second person working the effect.

When producing an effect that calls for masking off a section of the wall while applying paint right next to it (such as the stripes on page 151), always use low-tack painter's tape. You need a tape that is sticky enough to protect the surface from bleed, but not so sticky that it will rip off the paint underneath. Press down the edges firmly, apply only a thin coat of paint to prevent leakage, and build up the color with an additional coat if desired. Remove the tape immediately so that you can wipe away any leaks that have occurred.

colorwash, >>
nostalgic living room, PAGE 83

Colorwashing is one of the most popular paint effects. It's the easiest way to reproduce an uneven finish similar to the look of colors that have been broken down or faded by the sun and time. This is a complementary wall finish for traditional and country homes where the mood is personal and unpretentious. The variations in shades of paint camouflage imperfections on the walls, but also act as an enhancement over walls that are very bumpy or cracked. If you have new drywall, a colorwashed effect will add instant depth and character.

To produce the effect, a colored glaze is rubbed randomly over the base coat and softened with a rag to blend the shades. For a subtle effect, the base coat and glaze should be fairly closely matched; on a paint chip, about two steps apart. For a more naïve or dramatic look, choose contrasting combinations such as blue over white, or red over green.

In the living room vignette, I wanted to build a nostalgic mood, where I envisioned a family being surrounded by happy memories, and curling up after a busy day to chat or read together. The yellow ocher colorwash contributes texture and warmth reminiscent of an Old World setting.

INSTRUCTIONS

For best results, prepare your surface following the preparation tips on page 139.

step 1. Apply 2 base coats of mustard or medium yellow paint to the wall, and let it dry for 4 hours.

step 2. Mix a yellow ocher–colored glaze, 1 part latex paint to 3 parts water-based glazing liquid. This should be a darker shade of yellow than the base coat.

step 3. Work in 3- or 4-square-foot sections (see A Professional Finish, page 140). Roll the glaze over the first section randomly, leaving some patches with very little or no glaze at all.

step 4. With a soft, clean rag, dab at and rub the glaze to blend and soften.

step 5. Move to the next section and repeat steps 3 and 4 until the wall is finished, making sure to blend the lines between the sections before the glaze dries.

<< faux-stone **blocks,** nostalgic bathroom, PAGE 76

Imitating the look of a stone block wall with paint is an imaginative way to add historic charm to a kitchen, entrance hall, or European-style bathroom. Stone has a reputation for being cold, but when painted in warm shades of gray, beige, and yellow, the opposite is true.

When measuring and marking out the blocks, consider your room's dimensions and keep the blocks in proper scale. For a small bathroom or vestibule, a good size block is 16 inches by 12 inches. This technique requires playing with the glazes until you find your own method. There are many ways to get good results.

INSTRUCTIONS

For best results, prepare your surface following the preparation tips on page 139.

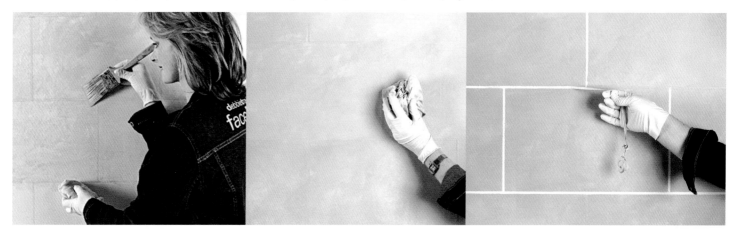

step 1. Apply 2 base coats of cream or off-white paint, and let dry overnight. This will be not only the base color for the added stone colors but also the color of the grout.

step 2. Measure and mark off the blocks, using a pencil and ruler or a chalk line. Use a level or T-square to keep the lines straight. Stagger the blocks as you would when building a real wall. Cover the lines with ¼-inch low-tack masking tape.

step 3. Mix 2 glazes, a sandy stone color and a pink stone color, in equal parts paint and glazing liquid.

step 4. Lightly brush on the sandy glaze, simultaneously dabbing out any brush strokes with a folded rag.

step 5. Apply the pink glaze sparingly, using the same method.

step 6. If needed, tiny flecks of white and gray can be applied with a sponge, being careful not to overdo your stone effect.

step 7. Remove the tape to reveal the grout lines. Any leakage under the tape adds to the realistic effect of the rough stone.

graphic design goes big... We are seeing a trend in larger-than-life decorating today; accent walls are brandishing blown-up geometric patterns, large color blocks, and oversized flowers. The appeal lies in their ability to be fearless, bold, and fun—a courageous alternative to update a bland room or highlight a focal wall. Large designs are available in wallpaper, but a similar effect can be produced with paint at a fraction of the cost. For stripes, rectangles, and squares, all you need are measuring and marking tools, including a level to keep lines straight, and a good supply of low-tack painter's tape. Magnified versions of intricate patterns, such as graphic designs and oversized flowers, can be applied with large stencils. Take a trip down to the library and check out some of the patterns from the '60s and '70s in older design books. Use today's flamboyant color palette for stunning results.

stenciling... One of the most enduring and endearing decorative arts, stenciling began as a craft and has moved into major design. The popularity of large shapes and motifs stretches our imaginations to come up with simple ways to replicate oversized patterns on our walls. You can buy large stencils, but they are expensive. By making your own, you are not only able to choose any pattern you want, you can custom cut it to fit the dimensions of your room. >> Libraries, books, magazines, and the Web are all sources for a favorite design. Use a photocopier to enlarge the pattern and trace it onto a piece of Mylar or clear plastic sheeting. Cut out the design carefully with an X-acto knife so that the edges are clean. Add registration marks to the top, bottom, and sides of your stencil as a guide to repositioning the pattern along the wall. For a large stencil, use both spray stencil adhesive and low-tack painter's tape to hold the stencil flat against the surface. To avoid smearing your work, wipe the back of the stencil clean of paint leaks before repositioning.

bamboo bath, >>
calm bath, PAGE 29

These simple stalks are easy to reproduce with paint. There are stencils available, or you can make your own.

step 1. Use a pencil or chalk and a ruler to mark off the direction and length of the stalks, with some crisscrossing as you see in the photograph. Mask off the design with low-tack painter's tape. Cut and stick down slightly irregular pieces of tape to demarcate the nodes that run around the bamboo horizontally at regular intervals.

step 2. Mix equal parts bamboo-colored paint and glazing liquid. I used a stencil brush to apply the glaze, dragging through the glaze to create the lines found in bamboo.

step 3. Remove the tape and wipe away any paint leaks immediately.

step 4. Cut a stencil in the shape of bamboo leaves and add them to the stalks.

turquoise lozenges, >>
cheerful dining room, PAGE 50

This retro design and color combination is based on the simple oval lozenge shape. The stencil pattern used to produce this fabulous wall represents the space in between the four corners of the oval shapes. Paint the pale turquoise base coat and let it dry overnight. Then you are ready to draw in guidelines and stencil on the dark blue spaces.

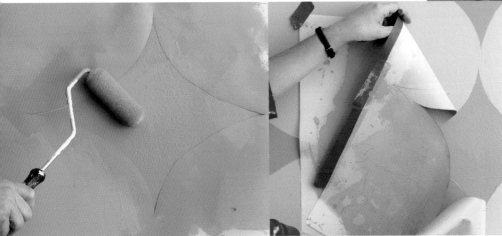

step 1. Make a template of the oval shape and cut out four ovals from a piece of paper or cardboard. Arrange them, edges touching in a square on a large piece of paper and draw around the corners to the halfway point of each oval. This is the stencil pattern you need. Trace the pattern onto a sheet of plastic or Mylar and cut out. Add registration marks at the top, bottom, and sides.

step 2. Draw a grid on the wall, dropping vertical lines at the sides of the ovals and horizontal lines that will cut through the middle of the ovals.

step 3. Line up the registration marks on the stencil with the wall grid. Adhere the stencil to the wall with spray adhesive and tape. Roll on the dark turquoise paint.

step 4. Remove the stencil immediately and wipe off any paint that may have leaked under the stencil onto the wall.

step 5. Wipe off any paint from the back of the stencil and move to the next position, being sure not to smudge the work you have already done.

<< floating flowers,
cheerful bedroom, PAGE 59

I photocopied and enlarged a picture of a single poppy to make this stencil. After the lilac base coat was on, I made a large grid of vertical and horizontal lines as a guide to stagger the poppies in a symmetrical pattern. Use chalk since it is easy to wipe off. One line of poppies is positioned at the point where the lines cross. On the next row, the poppies are at midpoints from the line above.

bath bubbles, >>
cheerful bath, PAGE 55

Bubbles give the illusion of lightness and air. There is an effervescent quality about their free movement that is cheerful and bright. I cut out four bubble stencils, each a different size, and used nontraditional colors—gold, mustard, yellow-green, and white—to paint in the shapes. They were applied randomly, some overlapping each other.

<< moroccan leaf,
dramatic bedroom, PAGES 108–9

This striking accent wall connotes the power of color and simple graphic design. The large Moroccan leaf motif appears to float randomly over the bed, as if blown by a tropical breeze. To heighten the impression of motion, the turquoise leaf is stenciled at different angles.

damask unplugged, >>
dramatic dining room, PAGE 115

The inspiration for this pattern came from a tapestry design. The enlarged pattern was stenciled onto the wall, turned randomly so that the shapes never seem to repeat. The base coat is white, and lemon yellow paint is rolled over the stencil for a dramatically bright and fresh finish. Experiment with other color combinations such as brown and orange, or green and pink, and the mood changes.

shadow blocking >> The trick behind shadow blocking is the contrast between gloss and matte sheens. Light reflects off glossy and metallic surfaces, making them advance and appear lighter in color. A matte surface absorbs light, producing the opposite effect. As the natural light in a room moves throughout the day, and incandescent lights are turned on in the evening, the colors will shift and change continually. >> You can create a shadow effect by alternating matte and high-gloss sheens of the same paint color, or painting in matte and blocking with high-gloss varnish.

<< metallic-glaze shadow blocks,
calm living room, PAGE 20

In this vignette, I chose to enhance the neutral brown walls by blocking off big squares and treating them with a golden metallic glaze. To keep the room airy, the squares should be on the large side and adjusted to the height of the wall—these are 22 inches. The wall was measured and marked off in an oversized grid, and then alternate squares were taped and filled with metallic glaze. Although the fireplace wall has the same finish, the angle of natural light dramatically changes the colors of the two walls.

INSTRUCTIONS

For best results, prepare your surface following the preparation tips on page 139. The walls were given 2 base coats of dark taupe-brown paint.

step 1. Divide the height of the wall by 4 or 5 to get the dimensions for the squares that will be in scale for your room. The larger the square, the more subtle and serene the outcome. Ours are 22 inches. Measure and mark off squares using a ruler and chalk line. Use a level or T-square to keep them straight.

step 2. Tape off alternate squares with low-tack painter's tape. Press down firmly along the edges of the tape.

step 3. Apply a thin coat of the translucent metallic glaze with a roller, starting in the middle of the square, and then feather it out so the glaze is not too heavy on the edges in order to avoid leakage under the tape.

step 4. Remove the tape immediately and clean up the edges.

stripes . . . If you are unsure about how to embellish your present décor, you need look no further than stripes; they will take you any place you want to go. There is no mood that cannot be enhanced by stripes in one of their many forms. The endless combination of colors and sizes range from straight-laced to wild and wacky, with lots of room in between for glamorous, relaxed, cheerful, and unpretentious. I have offered an alternative color combination for the striped patterns on these pages. >> Stripes alter our perception of space; our eyes have a tendency to follow lines, so vertical stripes make a room appear taller and horizontal stripes give the illusion of more space. >> For the subtlest impression, choose colors that are close, or try a shadow stripe (see Shadow Blocking on page 148). >> Painting stripes is easy, but there is a certain amount of measuring, marking, and taping that does take patience. To reword a helpful homily from my carpenter friends, measure twice, paint once. For best results, prepare your surface following the preparation tips on page 139. Always use low-tack painter's tape, and see A Professional Finish on page 140.

<< jagged stripes,
cheerful living room, PAGE 56

INSTRUCTIONS

step 1. Measure the width of the wall
and divide by the number of
striped patterns you want, so that
you can space them evenly
across the wall. These are about
18 inches apart. Use a plumb line
to mark off straight vertical lines.

step 2. You will need 1- and 2-inch-wide,
low-tack painter's tape. Rip down
one edge of the 2-inch-wide strip
of tape to make a jagged line.
Apply the tape as shown in the
photograph; from left to right,
1-inch tape, 1-inch space (pale
pink stripe), 1-inch tape, 4 inches
to the right-hand edge of the
jagged tape.

The pale pink stripe has been painted in. Now
fill in the jagged stripe with dark pink paint.

step 3. Remove the tape immediately and wipe off any
leaks. If the paint has dried, you can touch up
with the green paint.

alternative >> Try a white wall with a thin black
stripe and a silver metallic jagged stripe for a modern
and sophisticated mood with a humorous twist.

horizontal stripes, >>
dramatic living room, PAGE 116

When you are applying light and dark stripes, paint the light color as the base coat.

Let the white base coat dry overnight. Measure the wall from top to bottom and divide by 5 to get an even measurement for the wide bands. Use a level to ensure that your lines are straight. Use low-tack painter's tape to mask off, and fill in with dark blue paint.

alternative >> Try a wine red base coat with golden metallic translucent glaze over alternate bands for a traditional and elegant mood.

<< vertical triplet stripes,
nostalgic dining room, PAGE 85

These stripes are each 1 inch wide. Using 1-inch, low-tack painter's tape, mask off and paint the 2 outer dark red stripes first. Remove the tape and let the paint dry for at least 4 hours (overnight is safer, since you are going to tape over this fresh paint). Now tape over the dark red stripes and fill in the center gold stripe.

alternative >> Try a raspberry wall with turquoise outer and black inner stripes for a dramatic and high-spirited mood.

gingham, >>
nostalgic bedroom, PAGE 81

INSTRUCTIONS

Mix 2 blue glazes, one more transparent than the other. The glaze for the vertical stripes is 1 part blue paint to 3 parts glazing liquid. The glaze for the horizontal stripes is 1 part blue paint to 4 parts glazing liquid.

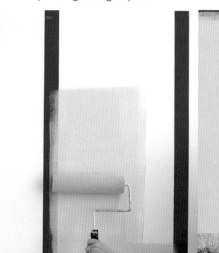

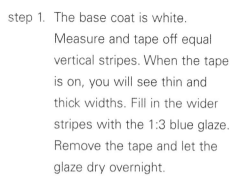

step 1. The base coat is white. Measure and tape off equal vertical stripes. When the tape is on, you will see thin and thick widths. Fill in the wider stripes with the 1:3 blue glaze. Remove the tape and let the glaze dry overnight.

step 2. Measure and tape off the horizontal stripes and apply the 1:4 blue glaze with a roller. It needs to be applied very smoothly in several sweeps; feather into the corners with a brush. You don't want to see roller lines. As the second glaze goes over the first, you get a darker shade, which creates the gingham effect.

alternative >> Try a sage-green background with dark green and red stripes. This unrestrained mood is traditional fun for a den.

metallic leaf and foil >> Metallic accents have been used for centuries to convey a mood of elegance and luxury. The luminous quality of gold, silver, copper, and brass resonates alone or alongside any color and material. Gilding is an art form familiar to us for its use on frames and ornately carved furniture. Gold or silver leaf is very expensive; however, imitation metallic leaf is available at art and craft stores at a more reasonable price. It's impossible to duplicate the unique glitter and gleaming qualities that radiate from metal leaf when it is applied to any surface.

<< silver leaf squares,
calm dining room, PAGE 25

INSTRUCTIONS

For best results, prepare your surface following the preparation tips on page 139. The walls were given 2 base coats of pale amethyst latex paint. The Asian-inspired stencil consists of 4 squares, a design often seen on Japanese kimonos.

step 1. Position the stencil on the wall using spray adhesive and low-tack painter's tape. Apply size (gilding glue) inside the stencil squares and let it dry until it is clear and tacky to the touch.

step 2. Gently place the silver leaf sheets on the squares, one at a time, and use a soft brush to smooth them out.

step 3. Remove the stencil and use the soft brush to wipe away any loose bits of leaf.

molding, trim, and panels...

To spruce up rooms that lack architectural detail or to create an eye-catching design flow throughout an open plain space (see Jodi and Luigi's home on page 102), there is a vast selection of moldings and trimwork available at hardware and lumber stores. Crown moldings, chair and plate rails, window and door trim, and baseboards all add individual character and enhanced style to a room. They come in lengths of wood, medium-density fiberboard, plastic, or foam, and are designed to be painted. (Solid wood can be stained to highlight the natural grain.) The surface of a molding or trim can be flat or curved, and some have a raised pattern, such as dentil molding.

crown molding runs around the top of the wall and should be kept in proportion to the height of the ceiling. For a 9-foot wall, a 4- to 6-inch-wide molding will produce a well-balanced impression. Use a miter box and saw to make neat, professional-looking cuts to join the pieces together.

a chair rail is a length of trim applied to the wall about 3 or 4 feet from the floor. It is a popular feature of both Victorian and country decorating, and is a good way to break up high walls. Always measure and mark the position of the rail up from the baseboard, since walls are seldom even. It is customary to paint the rail and lower wall one color, but there are many alternatives, such as wood paneling or wainscoting, tin panels or embossed wallpaper. Either hang wallpaper or paint the area above the rail in a lighter, contrasting shade.

a plate rail is designed with an indentation into which you rest the edge of plates lined up for display. The rail runs close to the top of the wall, usually about 18 to 24 inches from the ceiling. As with the chair rail, the trim breaks up the wall, offering many decorating options.

baseboard runs around the bottom of the wall. In most homes built after the '70s, baseboard is only about 3 inches high and not worth highlighting. If you want to add visual weight or interest to the lower walls, build up the height of the baseboard. Either apply a single board that is 6 or 8 inches high, or build up an architecturally interesting baseboard by piecing together different molding widths and designs. Fill in any gaps with pre-mixed plaster filler, prime all the sections, and then paint for a cohesive finish.

trim is a versatile tool for restyling flat-faced doors. It is easy to cut to size. Apply to the surface with carpenter's adhesive and secure with brads. Instead of replacing the lower kitchen cabinets in Glenn's kitchen (see page 95), we nailed on border trim to the doors, and modernized them with stunning charcoal gray paint.

door-casing trim, ⅝-inch thick and 1 inch wide, was applied in a lattice pattern to transform Olive's breakfast nook into a sunny garden setting (see page 67). To make the lattice design, mark off a grid with a pencil, measuring tape, and a chalk line. Use a plumb line to ensure the vertical lines are straight. Make the job easy by painting the lattice strips before they are installed. Then nail them over the grid lines, first all the verticals, followed by the horizontals.

A bit of trim and a good paint or stained finish can transform inexpensive materials into their more costly cousins. In Shelley's bedroom (see page 47), 1-inch by 2-inch strips were nailed over the seams of birch wall panels. The walls were then stained a deep, rich brown that imitates the look of exotic teak.

For Debbie's plantation bedroom (see page 89), the lower walls were paneled with 3-foot-wide sections of Masonite. We ran trim down the seams and along the top, and painted the panels glossy white for a classic colonial look.

how do
you choose
the homes for
Facelift?

what
happens
if the
homeowner
dislikes
the job?

does the
homeowner
have a say in
the design?

Go to our Web site, www.debbietravisfacelift.com, and tell us an interesting story or reason why your beloved deserves this Facelift.

it's rare but
we can
take care
of it . . .

occasionally,
but debbie's
the boss

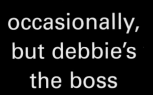

resources

Debbie Travis Specialty Collections, a line of specialty products such as glaze, stone-finish stucco, and more, are perfect for the contemporary, elegant interior. Available through The Painted House Web site (www.painted-house.com), by calling our toll-free number (1-800-932-3446), or through Martin & Associates (1-800-204-6278).

Accessories
Robert Allen
www.robertallendesign.com
United States: (800) 333-3777
Canada: (800) 363-3020
Vibrant, colorful, and sophisticated textiles for every interior, as seen in the mood vignettes throughout this book.

Caban
www.caban.com
Everything for the home, from dining and bathing to outdoor entertaining, as seen throughout this book.

Floors
Benchmark Carpet
www.benchmarkcarpet.ca
(416) 752-5554

Forbo Linoleum
www.themarmoleumstore.com
(866) marmoleum
Glenn's kitchen floor design was custom cut from linoleum tiles,
pages 95 and 97.

LSI North America Ltd.
www.lsitile.com
Vinyl flooring, Gun Metal #5013, in Karen's kitchen, page 121.

Smoothcorp
www.ifloor.com
NovaLinoleum, linoleum "floating" floor in Olive's kitchen, page 63.

Stencil Systems Decorative Concrete
United States:
www.stencilsytems.com
(888) 423-7778
Canada:
www.stencilsystems.net
(866) 483-6942
Faux-flagstone concrete floor in Toby and DJ's cabana, page 126.

Tilmar Internationale Inc.
www.tilmar.ca
Subway tiles for kitchen backsplash and counter in Olive's kitchen,
page 63.

Torlys
www.torlys.com
(800) 461-2573
Uniclic cork floor, Merlot, Sigal's den, page 32; Uniclic cork floor, African Ivory, Emma's apartment, page 72; Uniclic laminate floor, Summit Series in Oak Chestnut, Debbie's bedroom, page 89; Uniclic laminate floor in oak and Jatoba, Marilyn's living room, page 100.

Landscaping
Torizuka Landscaping
Ontario, Canada
(905) 780-0644
Kim Nakawatase designed and supervised the garden construction for Toby and DJ's cabana, page 124.

Paint and Walls
DuROCK
www.durock.com
(888) 238-6345
Spacco wall compound used on Sigal's den wall, page 33; Glenn's kitchen faux-brick archway, page 96; Luigi's fireplace surround, page 103. Venetian plaster used on fireplace in Shelley's bedroom, page 47.

Farrow and Ball
Traditional Paper and Paint
www.farrow-ball.com
United States: (845) 369-4912
Canada: (416) 920-0200
Wallpaper, St. Antoine #926, in Debbie's bedroom, page 89.

Lumigraf
www.lumigraf.ca
Orange translucent plastic sheeting is Lumigraf "California Sunset-A," Flamboyant Facelift, page 121.

Masterpieces Studio
www.masterpiecesstudio.com
(416) 781-5588
Jim Connelly and Peter de Sousa are specialists in paint and plaster faux finishes and specialty painting of all kinds. For the transfer foil used on page 132, contact Masterpieces.

Para Paints
www.para.com
All the rooms are painted with colors chosen from our friends at Para Paints.

index